Making and Arranging Silk Flowers

ANNE HAMILTON AND KATHLEEN WHITE

Flower Arranging and Flower Arranging Text by Sandra Munro
Foreword by Mary Law

 Sterling Publishing Co., Inc.   New York

For David and Norman
Pauline, Colin, Lesley-Anne and Steven
Brian, Graeme and Yvonne

Sincere thanks to Sandra – it was great working with you.

With grateful thanks for all their assistance to –
Anne McClarence & Elaine Vanston
Sandra Gilchrist
Jennifer and Lynne

Eucalyptus Method 2 on page 60 designed by Elaine Vanston

Published in 1990 by Sterling Publishing Company, Inc.
387 Park Avenue South, New York, N.Y. 10016

ISBN 0-8069-7286-6

First published in the U.K. in 1988 under
the title *Silk Flowers* by Merehurst Press, London.
© 1988 by Merehurst Limited
This edition published by arrangement with
Merehurst Press. Available in the United States,
Canada and the Philippine Islands only.
Distributed in Canada by Sterling Publishing
c/o Canadian Manda Group, P.O. Box 920, Station U
Toronto, Ontario, Canada M8Z 5P9

Library of Congress Cataloging-in-Publication Data

Hamilton, Anne.
    [Silk Flowers]
    Making and arranging silk flowers/Anne Hamilton and Kathleen
White: flower arranging and flower arranging text by Sandra Munro;
foreword by Mary Law.
        p.   cm.
    Reprint. Originally published: Silk flowers: making and arranging
ribbon flowers. London: Merehurst Press, 1988.
    1. Silk flowers.   2. Flower arrangement.   I. White, Kathleen.
    II. Munro, Sandra.   III. Title.
TT890.7.H36   1990
745.594'3--dc20   90–35918
                                                                CIP

10 9 8 7 6 5 4 3 2 1

Edited by Alison Leach
Photography by Steve Lee, assisted by Cliff Morgan
Typeset by Angel Graphics
Color Separation by Fotographics Ltd, London-Hong Kong
Printed by New Interlitho S.p.A., Milan, Italy

Contents

Foreword

This book brings together the creativity of ribbon flowers executed to a high standard of perfection and the artistry of a very talented flower arranger. It will be an enticement to all practically minded people. The step-by-step instructions and clear illustrations will ensure that the readers obtain the desired results, while the well-produced photographs of so many flower arrangements in a wide variety of settings demonstrate the usefulness of these lovely handmade flowers.

The three friends of mine who have produced this book have nature and natural plant materials very close to their hearts. Their interest stems from the beauty of the surroundings in which they live and from the inspiration of their own gardens. It has enabled them to combine their talents and produce this book for an artistic and imaginative readership. I am delighted to welcome this book for the sheer joy its beauty will bring to so many people.

MARY R. LAW, Past Chairman of the Scottish Association of Flower Arrangement Societies

Introduction

Around 1960, a Japanese lady who lived near a textile factory discovered that she could make lovely flowers from some of the discarded material from the factory. She began to sell her flowers and, after some time, her fame spread and she was asked to demonstrate her skill to others. Eventually, a manufacturer agreed to supply her with material directly and became interested in the following she had created. With her advice, the manufacturer began to make ribbons specially for flowermaking. Enthusiasm for this craft spread throughout Japan and later through the whole of the Far East.

Some years later, I heard about this craft by accident. My interest in flowermaking began while I was living in Hong Kong, with my husband and four young children. I had some time free in the mornings and decided to take a craft class. With my friend Magda Ounsworth, I booked for 'Ribbon Flowermaking'. Neither of us knew what to expect.

We found the class very interesting and especially enjoyed working with the beautiful ribbons used in making the flowers. Our enthusiasm increased and we took numerous more advanced classes. In the meantime, our friends had seen the flowers we had made and because of their interest, Magda and I decided to run classes ourselves. For the convenience of our pupils and to satisfy our own requirements, we purchased the special ribbons, wires, stamens and other materials in bulk from the manufacturers' agents.

To further our skills, we decided to go to Japan to take a residential course at a design school. This took a great deal of organization, but when we finally started the course, it proved to be both interesting and exacting. We were fortunate enough to be taken on tours of the factories producing the superb flowermaking ribbons and also attended exhibitions and demonstrations of flowermaking, taking the opportunity to find out about Ikebana, the Japanese floral craft. Attending a class on Ikebana as observers, we were advised that seven years is the average time a student must attend classes to be regarded as having a good basic knowledge of the subject.

Some time later, we negotiated an agreement with the leading manufacturer to be their sole agents in Britain. We had already decided that we should try to introduce this fascinating craft into Britain. Our families were to return home shortly and we had already established that we would not be able to obtain many of the items we needed from suppliers in the UK. In preparation for our return, we formed a company through which to trade in flowermaking materials. We chose the name Hamilworth, combining a part of each of our surnames.

In 1976, both Magda and I returned to Britain with our families and, after the settling-in period, set about developing our business as teachers and suppliers in ribbon flowermaking. Initially, we operated from our own attics and spare bedrooms, but as time went on we obtained business premises to store the increasing quantities of materials and to act as a despatch centre for wholesale and mail order trade. I had managed to interest my sister Kathleen and she too started classes and built up a substantial following. In 1984, Magda retired from the business and Kathleen has taken over Magda's share, operating from Chesterfield where she lives. Hamilworth's centre of operations is in Dumbarton in the west of Scotland.

Little did we think, in the early days, what could be the result of our enthusiasm for the ribbons, in their superb textures and glorious colours. The craft of ribbon flowermaking now attracts interest worldwide. Many of the items used in flowermaking are also in demand for other crafts, such as ribbon picture-making and sugarcraft. We know from experience that craft enthusiasts are only too eager to learn new tricks and as the interest in this craft increases, so too does the availability of the materials.

Kathleen and I are very keen gardeners and thoroughly enjoy fresh flowers and foliage. We have found that making artificial flowers has caused us to look more closely at their natural models, and we also enjoy the two things as separate interests, with their own pleasures and rewards. Silk and fabric flowers are gaining in popularity, however, and they can be used as substitutes for fresh flowers for special reasons. Many brides are now choosing a wedding bouquet of silk flowers because they can select the perfect colours and keep the flowers as a memento of the wedding day.

This book covers the whole range of flowermaking, from instructions for making the individual flowers to advice on arranging them and forming posies, gifts and accessories from your own flower selections. We hope it will enable you to match our enjoyment of this fascinating craft.

ANNE HAMILTON

Equipment and Materials

The basic equipment needed for silk and ribbon flowermaking is not specialized and consists of items which you probably have already for other purposes or can obtain quite easily. The marking and cutting equipment is as follows:

TRANSPARENT PLASTIC RULER marked with metric or metric/Imperial measurements.

PENCIL to mark measurements on the ribbons. Choose one which is neither too hard nor too soft, to avoid either scoring the ribbon surface or discolouring it with the pencil lead.

CRAFT SCISSORS with wire-cutting edges at the centre of the blades. Alternatively, you can equip yourself with medium-sized sharp scissors and a separate pair of wire cutters. Pliers are occasionally useful for bending heavy stem wires to shape and these often incorporate wire-cutting blades.

For texturing petals, you can obtain a special set of heads that can be fixed to a soldering iron (see page 9), but much of the texturing can be done by hand if necessary.

Making flowers from silk

Fabric flowers are commonly called silk flowers although often the fabric from which they are made is not real silk. The examples shown in this book are made from specially manufactured flowermaking ribbons. If you wish to create the flowers from silk, it is necessary to treat the material to prevent it from fraying, using the following recipe: Boil 900ml (30fl oz/1.9 US pints) of water in a saucepan. Mix 15g (½oz) starch with 1 teaspoon of water. Add to the boiling water and stir until it thickens. Leave to cool slightly and add 20g (¾oz) glue. Brush the mixture over the silk.

Flowermaking ribbons

The materials used to make the flowers illustrated are ribbons of various weights and textures: all consist of man-made fibres and are treated to resist fraying. Their qualities are specially designed for flowermaking and they should be obtained from a craft shop or by mail order. Hair and dressmaking ribbons are not always acceptable substitutes as some are likely to fray easily and may not give the required effect.

Flowermaking ribbons are available in a wide range of colours and finishes, so that almost any type of flower can be simulated.

ACETATE RIBBON is satin-faced on one side and matt-textured on the other. It is a firmly woven ribbon with a resin finish. It is normally used to show the satin side but the matt side is sometimes displayed to create particular effects. Green acetate is frequently used for leaves and sepals, and the lovely yellows, pinks and reds are ideal for rose petals.

Shaded acetate ribbon is also available, which has two bands of colour running lengthwise. One band is white or cream and the other a stronger hue. The colours merge at the centre of the ribbon.

LANTERN RIBBON is a firm acetate ribbon with pre-cut vertical slits which enable it to be used for making very fine petals and effects of loose fringing. It is also used to make lantern decorations (see page 115).

SILKY RIBBON is the most versatile flowermaking material, used for a wide variety of petals, florets, buds and leaves. It is a fine, lightweight ribbon available in a wide range of beautiful colours.

There are various types of silky ribbon which are used to imitate the particular colours and textures of natural flowers. Shaded silky ribbon has two colour bands running lengthwise which merge at the centre of the ribbon. One band is white or cream and the other a distinct colour. There is also a version of this ribbon with very subtle colour gradation from light to dark and a decorative metallic shaded ribbon with woven-in gold or silver lurex threads.

Two-colour silky ribbon is similar to the shaded ribbon but the bands are both distinct colours, again merging at the centre, so the colour variation is not necessarily from light to mid-tone or dark. This is available in two degrees of colour gradation, one slightly more subtle than the other.

Another variation of silky ribbon is a beautiful marble-effect shading of the colours.

VELVET SILKY RIBBON has a smooth pile, or nap, on one side and should be used to show the velvet side. It is used to imitate the richness of texture in some natural petals, such as those of the magnolia.

ORGANDY RIBBON is finer than silky, available in plain colours and in shaded colours with one band of white or cream.

POPLIN RIBBON is firmer than silky but less heavy than acetate. It is available in plain and shaded colours and has a silky sheen.

COTTON RIBBON is slightly heavier than poplin and has a matt finish. It is available in a range of lovely colours.

FLOCKED RIBBON is an acetate ribbon with a velvet pile, used with the velvet side displayed.

SEAL RIBBON is a relatively heavy ribbon of ribbed velvet on one side.

Pre-formed materials

Tiny florets, such as those in forget-me-not flowerheads, are available in pre-cut form and they can be shaped by moulding with a heated tool (see page 9). These pre-cut florets are very useful for making up delicate sprays and posies to be inserted as fillers in arrangements or in decorative sprays made mainly with larger flowers.

Individual pre-formed leaves are available in different ribbon types for certain flowers. Rose leaves are made from green velvet, metallic or silky ribbon, chrysanthemum leaves from velvet ribbon, and poppy leaves from seal ribbon.

Ivy, caladium, geranium and spotted laurel leaves are obtainable in the form of printed rolls. The individual leaves are cut to shape and reinforced with wire before they are applied to a flower stem or inserted in an arrangement. The printed leaf patterns, as well as providing a realistic effect in individual flower stems or sprays, contribute a useful extra element to the design of a silk flower arrangement.

Stamens

There are several different types of ready-made flower stamens – round- or pointed-tipped, dull, pearlized, frosted, sparkle or gloss finish – in various sizes and a range of colours. Stamens are usually supplied as double-headed strings which can be cut or doubled over to form short-stemmed stamens, with the exception of lily stamens, which have long stems and a single head.

Construction materials

The following materials are in constant use when you are making

5

silk flowers and it is advisable to acquire a good stock of the items you will need.

Stem tape
This material is commonly used by florists and is directly adaptable to silk flowermaking. It is a strong, flexible paper tape impregnated with a substance that makes it self-adhesive. Stem tape is used to cover stem wires and to fasten components of the flower together. There are several shades of green and brown for use on stems, and also a range of lovely colours. From time to time you will need stem tape matching the flower colour in order to neaten flower bases, bind stamen stems and make buds or flower centres.

Wires
Several different thicknesses of wire are used in silk flowermaking. They are specified in the flowermaking instructions by the British Standard Gauge number: you can find the equivalent metric and Imperial measurements of thickness by consulting the chart below. The higher the gauge number, the finer the wire.
UNCOVERED WIRES are used in gauges 30, 22, 20 and 18. The 30-gauge wire is relatively fine and is used for wiring petals and fastening flowers and leaves to stems. The lower gauges are mainly used as stem wires. All these wires are sold in standard lengths.
COVERED WIRES are available in standard gauges but the wire is covered with paper of a particular colour. Green or white covered wires are available in gauges 33, 30, 28, 26 and 24. Colours including light green, pink, red, wine red, beige, brown, blue and yellow are available in 26-gauge only.
PADDED CRAFT WIRE in 16-gauge is useful for making thick stems and simulating branches, if covered with an appropriate colour of stem tape.

Adhesive materials
Because you are working with fine materials and often on a small scale, it is essential that adhesive materials are not only effective in their adhesive property but also give a clean finish.
FLOWERMAKING ADHESIVE is a white polyvinyl compound which becomes transparent as it dries. Proprietary brands are available in small bottles or tubes, or in tins. However, you will need to use very little at one time and it is important that the container is properly sealed when not in use.
DOUBLE-SIDED ADHESIVE TAPE is obtained by the roll, like ordinary adhesive tape, but because it is a very fine film which is adhesive on both sides, it is backed by a paper strip. This must be removed after the tape is applied to one component and just before another component or material is attached. It is effective in securing together two pieces of ribbon, with or without a reinforcing wire in between. It is available in 5mm ($\frac{3}{16}$in), 24mm ($\frac{15}{16}$in) and 36mm ($\frac{7}{16}$in) widths.

Basic Techniques

This chapter describes all the flowermaking techniques which recur in the instructions for individual flowers. These are the basic skills of silk flowermaking and if you are new to the craft, it may be helpful to try out these techniques before you start to make the flowers. Where a special technique is needed to create a particular effect, this is explained in the step-by-step instructions.

Cutting
Shapes can be cut from ribbon either freehand or by using a template. Freehand cutting is quicker and produces a more natural result. The use of templates is perfectly acceptable and is probably advisable with some of the more complicated shapes until you feel confident of cutting accurately. Templates of the main components of each flower are provided on pages 64 to 83.
   In order to reduce material wastage to a minimum, it is important to consider the most economical way of cutting the ribbon before you start making the flower. The width of many flowermaking ribbons is 72mm ($2\frac{13}{16}$in) and, wherever possible, the size given for a petal or leaf is calculated on a proportion of this measurement which will allow you to cut shapes side by side across the width of the ribbon. If you are working with ribbons larger or smaller than 72mm ($2\frac{13}{16}$in) width, it should be possible to make minor adjustments based on the template shape to achieve a petal or leaf of suitable size and proportions.
   For some single and multiple elements, such as narrow leaves or multi-tipped petals, the simplest way to cut them is to fold a large piece of ribbon into the appropriate number of sections and cut a single shape out of the folded layers.
   When cutting a petal or leaf, it is best to start at the tip. Follow the steps shown, turning the ribbon as indicated to arrive at the final outline. Keep the cutting action smooth; this is particularly important when cutting rounded shapes. Hold the scissors straight and, using the full length of the blades, feed the ribbon steadily into the scissors.

WIRE GAUGE MEASUREMENTS
All wire gauges referred to are British Standard gauges. If other standard gauges are used, the measurement of the wire should be checked against the following table and an equivalent used where necessary.

BRITISH STANDARD WIRE GAUGE	EQUIVALENT IN MILLIMETRES	EQUIVALENT IN INCHES
16	1.63	0.064
18	1.22	0.048
20	0.914	0.036
22	0.711	0.028
24	0.559	0.022
26	0.457	0.018
28	0.376	0.0148
30	0.315	0.0124
33	0.254	0.0100

CUTTING PETALS AND LEAVES

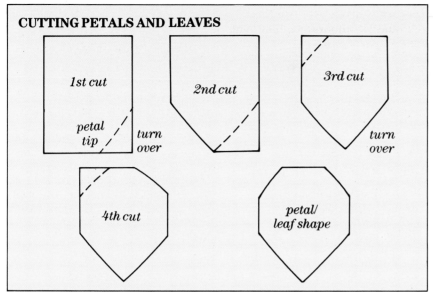

1st cut

petal tip / turn over

2nd cut

3rd cut / turn over

4th cut

petal/ leaf shape

Five-point fold

Many petals and calyces have five segments to the overall shape. It can be difficult to cut these freehand but there is a simple technique of folding the ribbon which simplifies the cutting and creates a uniform shape. The instructions (see below) are based on a 72mm (2¹³⁄₁₆in) square but you can adjust the dimensions throughout to work on a larger or smaller scale. With practice, you will find it easy to make the folds; it is advisable to try out the technique with thin paper before using the ribbon.

Where the five-point fold is used in making a particular flower, a diagram is provided marked with the cutting line for the individual component.

FIVE-POINT FOLD

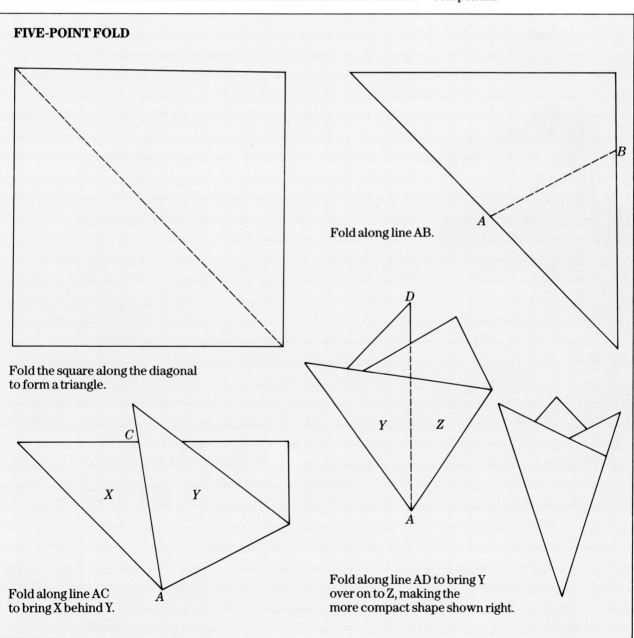

Fold the square along the diagonal to form a triangle.

Fold along line AB.

Fold along line AC to bring X behind Y.

Fold along line AD to bring Y over on to Z, making the more compact shape shown right.

Texturing

Flower petals and leaves show different qualities of form and texture which are part of their natural growth patterns. In ribbon flowermaking, special techniques of texturing are used to simulate these qualities, to give a natural-looking result in the finished flower. Several of these techniques can be done either by hand or using a heated tool designed for the purpose.

Stretching

Many flowers have frilled or fluted petals. To achieve this effect, stretch the ribbon just inside the edge of the petal between your fingers and thumbs. The most pronounced flare is achieved if the petal is damp. However, care is needed, as it is possible to tear the ribbon, especially when stretching on a cut edge.

Cupping

Cupping of petals, for example, in the rose or poppy, is best achieved if the petal is bias cut across the grain of the ribbon. Hold the centre of the petal between thumbs and forefingers and pull against the bias.

When wiring a cupped petal, emphasize the shape as you gather the ribbon at the base.

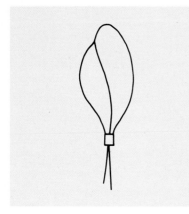

Rolling

Roll the edge of a petal over a short length of heavy wire or a fine knitting needle. Withdraw the wire and alternately roll and pull the curled edge until it automatically springs back into place when released. Rose petals require this effect.

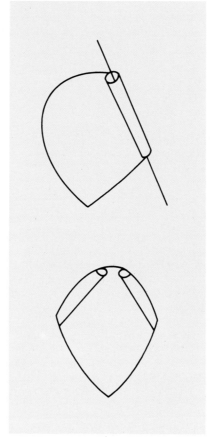

Curling

Petals, leaves and fringing can be curled by drawing the ribbon firmly across the closed blades of a pair of scissors.

Crinkling

In nature, many petals and leaves have a crinkled texture running across the whole surface. This can be created by either of two methods:
DAMP CLOTH METHOD Use a handkerchief or piece of lightweight cotton fabric. Dampen the cloth and spread it on the work surface. Fold the petal (or leaf) in half lengthwise and position it on the damp cloth. Fold the cloth down over the petal. Place the heel of one hand firmly on the covered petal. Gather the corner of the cloth in the other hand and pull slowly but firmly through 180 degrees, maintaining firm pressure on the petal.

If you are working with a thick material, such as flocked ribbon, it is best to use a heavier cloth; a damp facecloth is particularly effective.

SPIRAL TWIST METHOD Fold the petal or leaf in half along its length and twist it into a spiral. Hold it firmly to press in the crinkled texture, then open it right out.

Both of these methods should be applied ▸efore reinforcing a petal or leaf with wire, as the wire may be dislodged during the process. However, if the item is fully lined and the wire is secured between two layers of ribbon, the crinkling can be applied to the completed petal or leaf.

Tooling
A soldering iron fitted with special flowermaking heads can be used to texture petals and leaves. There are two mushroom heads for cupping medium-sized and large petals, and

a ball head for cupping small petals. A blade head is used for marking veins on petals or leaves. Of the two heads with curved tips, one is smooth for making a channel or curling a petal over on itself; the other is ridged for making a furrowed channel or parallel veins. The rose-petal curling head is a curved, pointed tool used for curling petal edges. The forget-me-not head is a small curved mould which can be impressed on the shape of very small pre-formed petals.

When using the heated tool, it is best to work on a heat-resistant tray or on a well-protected table or work surface. You will need a soldering iron stand or a heatproof dish and a soft fabric pad about 150mm (5⅞in) wide, filled with down or foam.

Select the head required and fit it to the shaft of the soldering iron. Make sure the screw is secure. Switch on the iron and leave it for a few minutes to heat.

When tooling a petal or leaf, lay the ribbon on the pad before applying the heated tool.

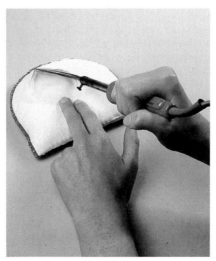

CUPPING Press the selected tool head on the ribbon for a few seconds. If the area to be cupped is large, move the head around a little to cover the area required.

VEINING Draw the blade head firmly along the ribbon to draw the line of the vein; usually, you should work from the outer edge towards the centre of the leaf or petal.

CHANNELLING Depending upon the position of the channel, draw the smooth curved head down the petal or leaf from top to bottom, or around the outer edge. If you move the tool slowly through the centre of the shape, the whole petal will curl over.

To make a ridged channel, draw the ridged curved head across the ribbon in the required position. This technique can also be used to mark parallel veins or to curl the whole petal over.

ROLLING AND CURLING Firmly stroke the edges of the petal with the rose-petal curling tool from the outer edge inwards.

MOULDING Simply hold the forget-me-not head on the petal to mould the shape.

It normally takes just a few seconds to texture with the heated tool heads and care must be taken not to burn the ribbon by holding the head on it for too long. When working with some intricately cut petals, it may be helpful to put one or two plain pins through them to anchor them in position on the pad.

When you finish working with a tool head, switch off the electricity supply to the tool, unscrew the head and put it into the heatproof dish to cool. Always leave the heated tool on a stand or in the heatproof dish until it has cooled completely.

Reinforcing and lining
It is often necessary to reinforce a petal or leaf because of its size, or the way it 'sits' on the flowerhead or stem. A simple way to do this is by sticking a wire on the back of the ribbon; this wire can then be gently curved to achieve the desired effect. Lining may be done to strengthen the ribbon or to provide a different texture on one side of a petal or leaf, for example, a silky lining on the underside of a velvet leaf.

Reinforcing
Cut a length of covered wire a little longer than the petal or leaf. Apply adhesive to the underside of the wire and lay this on the wrong side

9

of the piece of ribbon, starting about 5mm (³⁄₁₆in) from the top. Make sure the wire is on the side of the ribbon which will not be visible in the finished flower. Instructions for individual flowers state which is the correct side.

If an individual stem is required for a flower or leaf, cut the reinforcing wire to about twice the length of the petal or leaf shape and adjust the length when taping it to a main stem.

Strip-lining
To strip-line a petal or leaf, cut a narrow strip of ribbon to match the shape and apply narrow double-sided adhesive tape to this. Peel the backing paper from the tape and lay a piece of covered wire on it, about 5mm (³⁄₁₆in) below the top of the strip. Lay the wired strip on the petal or leaf and press down firmly to attach the adhesive tape.

Full-lining
In full-lining, a wire is sandwiched between two layers of ribbon which are stuck together with flowermaking adhesive or double-sided tape. The leaf or petal shape is cut after lining.

Lay double-sided adhesive tape over the whole area of one piece of ribbon, making sure it is on the wrong side if using velvet silky or acetate ribbon. Press the reinforcing wire down on the tape, then cover it with the second piece of ribbon and smooth this down firmly.

With fine or lightweight ribbons, it is not always necessary to attach the full shape of the lining piece. The reinforcing wire can be attached to a strip of double-sided tape running down the centre of the leaf or petal and the lining can also be attached to this strip only.

When positioning reinforcing wires on petals or leaves, make sure the top of the wire is at least 5mm (³⁄₁₆in) from the edge of the ribbon, otherwise it is noticeable in the finished flower. If using a heavy gauge wire for reinforcing, allow twice that measurement to ensure that the tip of the wire does not show.

Using adhesive
Flowermaking adhesive is specially formulated for use with ribbons. It cannot be softened once it has begun to dry, so it is essential to keep the lid on the container when you are not using the adhesive.

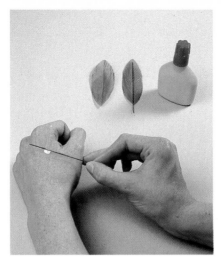

To apply the adhesive, put a small blob on a matchbox top, or on the back of your left hand if you are right-handed, or vice versa. Make a hook at the top of a piece of wire and use this as an applicator to transfer the adhesive to the ribbon. Be careful not to apply too much or the excess will ooze out between glued sections. If the ribbon pieces to be stuck together are large, then it is easier to squeeze the adhesive out of the bottle directly onto the centre of one piece and use the wire hook to spread it.

To stick two pieces of ribbon together, press them firmly between your fingers. To stick wire to ribbon, gently dot the underside of the wire into the blob of adhesive on your hand, so that only the underside of the wire is wet, position it on the ribbon and hold it in place for about 30 seconds.

Do not continue work with the wired ribbon until the adhesive has dried; this usually takes about 30 minutes.

Using double-sided adhesive tape
Double-sided tape is ideal for sticking two pieces of ribbon together, for example, when making fully-lined petals or leaves. The tape must be kept in a plastic bag when not in use, otherwise it will dry out and lose its adhesive property.

When making a fully lined leaf or petal, lay one piece of ribbon on the table or worktop and carefully place on it a strip of double-sided tape of the appropriate width and length. Press it down firmly, especially at the corners, and peel off the backing paper. Immediately place the second piece of ribbon on top, making sure that you apply it

smoothly. Do not remove the backing paper from the tape until you have the second piece of ribbon ready to be applied. The adhesive tape attracts dust and fibres very quickly and if left exposed will become dirty and lose its adhesion.

If you are applying a reinforcing wire to the ribbon, put this in place as soon as you remove the backing paper from the tape and cover it with the piece of lining ribbon immediately. Smooth down the ribbon to cover the wire cleanly.

When you are working with fine ribbons, a narrow strip of double-sided tape holds quite large pieces of ribbon together effectively. Lay a strip of 5mm (³⁄₁₆in) tape down the centre of the ribbon shape. Press down firmly, then remove the backing paper and place the second piece of ribbon on top. If this shape is to be reinforced with wire, lay the length of wire in position before the second piece of ribbon is applied.

Taping
Stem tape is used to cover bare wires and provide a neat finish to stems, and for fastening together several parts of a flower during construction. The tape is used full-width, half-width, and sometimes quarter-width. To make half-width tape, peel a few layers of tape from the roll, press them evenly together and cut lengthwise through the centre. If you require quarter-width tape, divide one of the batches of half-width tape again in the same way.

If you have never used stem tape before, it is best to practise using full-width tape. Stretch a short length at one end of the tape and lay it across the top of a stem wire. Squeeze the tape onto the wire. Hold

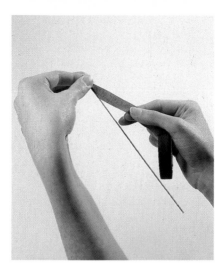

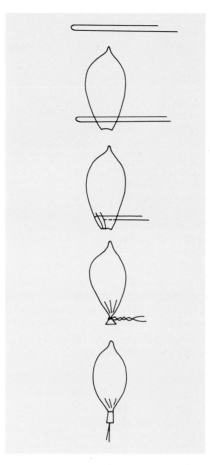

the wire in one hand and the tape in the other at an acute angle to the wire. Roll the wire into the tape, making sure that the tape is stretched as it is applied. This reduces the quantity of tape needed and makes a neat finish.

When assembling some flowers, or grouping flowers into a plant or spray, separate wires are taped together to form the main stem. To avoid the wires becoming twisted during taping, it is advisable to secure them first by rolling a little tape around all the wires at intervals up the stem. They will not then slip out of place or twist as you tape the whole stem.

Always keep stem tape in a plastic bag to prevent it from drying out.

Wiring

Four main methods of wiring are used to gather and secure the bases of petals or leaves, to assemble them in sequence, or to attach them to a stem. A fine and flexible wire is needed, usually 30-gauge wire.

Hairpin method

This is suitable for wide-based petals and leaves or those made from a thick material such as flocked or velvet silky ribbon.

Make a hairpin shape with 30-gauge uncovered wire (above right) and place this around the base of the petal or leaf, about 10mm (³⁄₈in) above the bottom edge of the ribbon. It is important to keep this allowance of ribbon even.

Starting from the left-hand side of the shape, make small, even gathers in the ribbon. It is important to maintain tension on the wires while doing this, which you can achieve by winding the wires around your fingers. Secure the petal by holding

the two lengths of wire tightly and turning the petal over to twist the wire. Bring the ends of the wire down to form a stem and tape for a length of about 20mm (¹³⁄₁₆in).

Wiring in sequence

It is often necessary to link petals together before arranging them on a stem. There are two methods of wiring in sequence.

SINGLE-ROW SEQUENCE (below right) Take two lengths of 30-gauge wire and hold them horizontally a little apart. Twist the two wires together towards one end, leaving about 100mm (3¹⁵⁄₁₆in) free at that side, with the greater length of the wires extending on the other side. Hold the greater lengths of wire slightly apart and insert a petal. Gather the base of the petal neatly. Hold the two lengths of wire firmly and turn the petal to secure the wire.

Open the wire back to one twist after the first petal and insert the second petal next to the first, making sure the allowance of ribbon below the wire is even. Repeat the

process of wiring until all the petals are secured by the wires. Each petal should slightly overlap the one before at the broadest part. When the sequence is complete, hold the wires firmly where the last petal is fastened and turn the linked petals to secure the wires. Do not cut the wires.

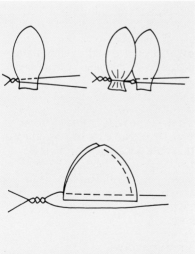

When making the Pompon Dahlia (page 45) and Spiky Dahlia (page 50), the wire is passed between the ribbon folds in the sequence wiring.

11

It is important to maintain tension in the wires, so wrap the long lengths around your fingers while gathering the petal bases.

Alternatively, you can apply this method using a single length of wire bent to form a loop at one end. Twist the looped end and insert the petals as described above. It may help to maintain tension on the wires if you hook your little finger into the loop of wire.

This method is suitable for wiring small numbers of petals, particularly if the petals themselves are small and delicate.

DOUBLE-ROW SEQUENCE Use 30-gauge wire to link the petals as described in the single-row sequence but create the double row by positioning the petals very closely together, alternately in front of or behind the one before.

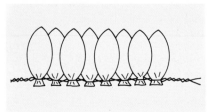

Twisting method
This is a method of securing individual components together and is particularly suitable for narrow-based petals or leaves. It is very useful when adding a leaf, calyx or bract directly to a stem or flowerhead.

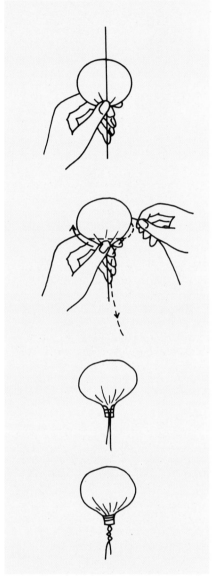

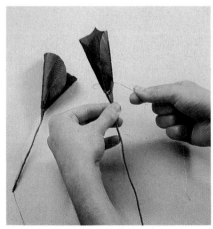

To join a leaf to a stem by this method (below centre), hold the base of the leaf against the stem and place a short end of 30-gauge wire against the leaf. Hold the wire end and leaf in position with your thumb and firmly wind the long end of 30-gauge wire once or twice around the stem. To secure the leaf, hold the long and short ends of wire together and twist them by turning the stem. Trim the wires and cover the ends with stem tape.

The same procedure may be used to attach petals to a flower centre or stem tip.

Making flower centres
Some flower centres are almost concealed by the petals, while others are an important aspect of the flower's visual attraction. Whichever is the case, it is important to form the flower centre correctly as it is the basis of the way the petals are grouped and attached to the stem. Pre-formed stamens are used in most flower centres. Fringing is also frequently needed to create the right effect. The button centre is appropriate for flowers with flat, open faces. Special variations are given with the step-by-step instructions.

Stamen centre
Stamens are supplied as double-headed strings. Normally, to make a flower centre the stamen strings are folded in half and a piece of 30-gauge wire is passed through the loop to fasten them together. The two ends of the wire are secured by holding them firmly and twisting the

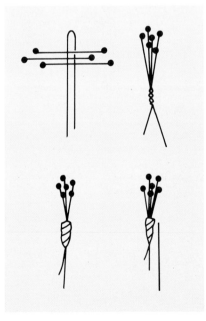

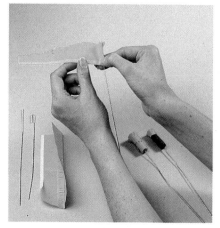

stamens, and are then neatened with stem tape, full- or half-width depending on the thickness of the bunch of stamens.

If a long stem is required for the stamen centre, one head is cut off the stamen string to utilize the full length. The cut ends of the stamens are secured by the twisting method (see opposite), using 30-gauge wire. The wired base is neatened with half-width stem tape.

Large stamens can be made from uncovered wire by taping the top of the wire with coloured stem tape to make a little ball, then taping down the wire to form the stamen stem. To make a cluster of wire stamens, tape or wire them together at the bottom of the stems.

Fringed centre
A piece of ribbon is fringed by cutting vertically from one long edge at narrow intervals, leaving an

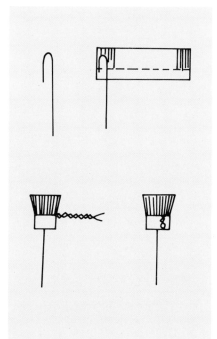

uncut base strip along the opposite edge of the ribbon. Place a piece of double-sided adhesive tape along the uncut strip (or this can be applied before you cut the fringing).

To attach a fringed centre to a stem, take a length of stem wire taped down about 30mm (1³⁄₁₆in) of its length, or use covered wire, and form the top of the wire into a hook. Remove the backing paper from the double-sided tape attached to the fringe, hook the wire into the fringe and squeeze tightly. Roll the fringed strip firmly and evenly around the wire hook, keeping the top and bottom edges level. Fasten the base with 30-gauge wire and tape over and down the wire with coloured stem tape.

Button centre
The size of the button depends upon the size of the flower but normally one slightly larger than a shirt button will do. Bend a length of 30-gauge wire into a hairpin shape and thread it through two holes in the button. Hold the two ends of wire under the button and twist the button to secure the wires. Cover the button completely with full-width stem tape in the appropriate colour. Join in a stem wire and secure the join with stem tape.

Thickening stems
It is sometimes necessary to thicken the full length of a stem, or the end near the flower centre, or at the leaf nodes, as for the carnation (see page 21). This can be done by applying several layers of stem tape, by adding more wires and taping them, or by winding 10mm (³⁄₈in) strips of tissue tightly around the taped stem. Tissue thickening should be finished by covering the stem with full-width stem tape.

Padded 16-gauge craft wire is

available which is ideal for the particularly heavy stems of bamboo, clivia and bird of paradise flowers.

Assembling
There are various methods of assembly which depend on the size and construction of the flower, and the number of components to be assembled.

Petals and leaves which have been wired and taped individually can be held in position around a flower centre or on a stem and taped in place directly with stem tape. It is not necessary to use wire to secure them.

Leaves or bracts which have not been individually wired are usually attached to a stem or flowerhead by the twisting method (see opposite).

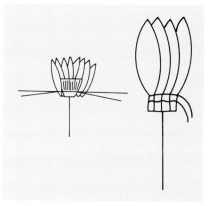

Petals wired in sequence are attached to the flower centre using the ends of the wires that link the petals, the flower centre being already attached to a stem wire. Hold the ring of petals around the flower centre, bring the short ends of wire down the flower stem and wrap the long ends right around petals and centre at the base of the flower, just above the wire linking the petals. Pull tightly and bring the short ends of wire up to meet the long ends. Twist the flowerhead to secure. Care should be taken to ensure that the allowances of ribbon at the petal bases are all smoothed downwards and that the ring of petals has been kept level. Trim the wires to different lengths so that they do not create a lumpy effect on the stem and cover them with stem tape.

When making very small flowers, such as the snowdrop, use only one long length of 30-gauge wire to secure the petals to the flower centre or stem. Pull as tightly as possible and hold the wire below the flowerhead while you turn the head to secure the wire. When taped, this makes a neat finish to the small flower.

13

Making Silk Flowers

The instructions for making each flower specify the best type of ribbon for achieving the required effect. In many cases silky ribbon can be substituted for the given material, but in the following cases you will only achieve the right result by using the same type of ribbon as shown in the instructions:

African Violet
Arum Lily
Easter Lily
Michaelmas Daisy
Pansy
Pompon Dahlia
Spider Chrysanthemum
Spiky Dahlia
Wallflower

Templates for the flower and leaf shapes and diagrams showing how to fold and cut the ribbon to make the required shapes follow the step-by-step instructions from page 64. The quantities of ribbon needed to make each flower as shown are listed on page 63.

AFRICAN VIOLET (Saintpaulia)

MATERIALS
Velvet silky or flocked ribbon in deep purple

Flocked ribbon in green

Lemon yellow stamens

Green stem tape

30-gauge wire

24-gauge green covered wire

Flowermaking adhesive

1 Cut 24mm ($^{15}/_{16}$in) squares of purple velvet ribbon, five for each flower and two for each bud. Cut one petal shape from each square and crinkle using the spiral twist method.

To make one flower, wire five petals together in single-row sequence, using 30-gauge wire, with velvet sides facing you. To make one bud, wire two petals together in sequence, velvet sides facing.

For each flower or bud, cut a stamen string in half and tape below the head with half-width stem tape to thicken.

Wrap stem tape around the end of a length of green covered wire to thicken it into a small closed bud. Continue taping down the stem.

2 With velvet pile on the inside, wrap the wired flower petals around the stamen. Secure by winding one long end of wire round the flower base, hold the wires together, twist the flowerhead and tape. Tape the flower to a length of green covered wire using half-width stem tape and open out the petals.

Repeat to make a second flower.

Assemble the bud in the same way but do not open the petals.

3 Cut a 36×40mm ($1^7/_{16}$×$1^9/_{16}$in) rectangle of green flocked ribbon and shape the leaf. Crinkle using the spiral twist method. Using flowermaking adhesive, stick a length of green covered wire to the

centre of the leaf on the shiny side. Tape the base of leaf and stem with half-width stem tape.

Cut smaller leaves from 24×30mm ($^{15}/_{16}$×$1^3/_{16}$in) and 20×26mm ($^{13}/_{16}$×$1^1/_{16}$in) rectangles. Arrange flowers, buds and leaves into a cluster and tape the stems together to finish.

If you wish to assemble a full plant, make at least nine flowers and four buds, and surround them with leaves in varying sizes, the smaller leaves at the centre of the plant.

ALSTROEMERIA

MATERIALS
Shaded poplin ribbon in deep pink/cream

Poplin ribbon in white

Silky ribbon in pale green

Deep pink stamens

Green stem tape

30-gauge wire

28-gauge white covered wire

20-gauge stem wire

Flowermaking adhesive

Felt-tip pens in yellow, brown and dark pink

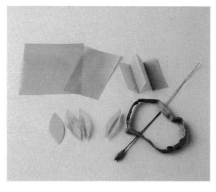

1 Cut three 24×45mm (¹⁵⁄₁₆×1¹³⁄₁₆in) rectangles of shaded poplin ribbon and shape petals A. Cut one 18×45mm (¹¹⁄₁₆×1¹³⁄₁₆in) rectangle of shaded poplin and cut one petal B. Cut two 18×45mm (¹¹⁄₁₆×1¹³⁄₁₆in) rectangles from white poplin ribbon and shape petals C.

With a felt-tip pen, colour top and bottom of both white petals to match the pink of the shaded ribbon. Use the yellow pen to colour the centre of each. Fleck these and petal B using the brown pen.

Using adhesive, stick a length of 28-gauge white covered wire down the centre of each petal. Tool down either side of the wire on all petals A using the ridged head. On petals B and C, tool down the wire.

shape of a closed bud. Continue taping down the wire stem.

Repeat to make a second bud.

Cut a 24×72mm (¹⁵⁄₁₆×2¹³⁄₁₆in) rectangle of pale green silky ribbon. Fold it in four widthways and cut out the leaf shape to make four leaves. Tool down the centres using the ridged head.

Tape the second flower, the two buds and the leaves to the main stem, varying the positioning and angles to create a natural effect. Tape to the end of the main stem to finish off.

ARUM LILY (Zantedeschia aethiopica)

1 Cut a 144×155mm (5¹¹⁄₁₆×6⅛in) rectangle from white acetate ribbon and shape the petal. On the matt side of the ribbon, tool with the smooth head around the outer curves about 5mm (³⁄₁₆in) from the edges.

Use the green crayon to colour the base of the petal on the matt side of the ribbon.

On the shiny side of the ribbon, starting from the base, attach a length of 5mm (³⁄₁₆in) double-sided tape about 45mm (1¹³⁄₁₆in) along the outer edge of the petal.

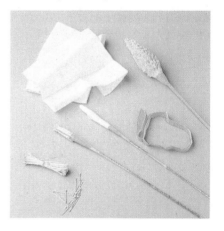

2 Assemble six stamens and cut off the heads at one end. Bind them together at the cut ends with 30-gauge wire.

Tape petals B and C around the stamen cluster. Tape petals A in the spaces between the B and C petals.

Attach a length of 20-gauge stem wire to the flower and continue taping the stem to the point where another flower or leaf is added.

Repeat to make a second flower.

3 Wrap half-width stem tape around one end of a length of 20-gauge wire to thicken it into the

MATERIALS

Wide acetate ribbon in white and green
Yellow stamens
Stem tape in green and yellow
18-gauge stem wire
Double-sided adhesive tape in 5mm (³⁄₁₆in) and 36mm (1⁷⁄₁₆in) widths
Flowermaking adhesive
Light green crayon
White tissue paper

2 Cut the stamen strings in half. Tape two lengths of 18-gauge wire together and thicken about 50mm (2in) at one end by binding with tissue paper. Cover the tissue with yellow stem tape.

Using adhesive, stick ten to fifteen stamens around the thickened tip. Apply a second ring of stamens just below the first and repeat the process to build up the centre of the flower evenly as shown. Neaten the base of the clustered stamens with yellow stem tape. Allow the adhesive to dry.

3 Remove the backing paper from the double-sided tape on the petal and wrap the petal firmly

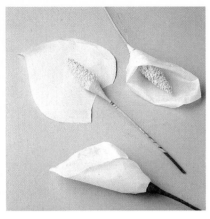

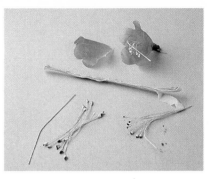

around the stamen centre, shiny side inwards. Press firmly to secure. Tape the base with green stem tape.

4 Cut two 144×210mm (5¹¹⁄₁₆×8¼in) rectangles of green acetate ribbon. Cover the matt side of one with double-sided tape.

Cover a length of 18-gauge wire with green stem tape. Attach the wire to the double-sided tape down the centre of the rectangle.

Lay the second rectangle shiny side up over the first and smooth it down. Cut out the leaf shape as shown, so that the reinforcing wire runs through the centre.

Mark the leaf veins using scissor blades or the tool blade head. Tape the leaf to the flower stem.

AZALEA

MATERIALS
Silky ribbon in orange/pink and green
Dark-tipped pink stamens
Stem tape in pink and green
5mm (³⁄₁₆in) double-sided adhesive tape
30-gauge wire
26-gauge green covered wire
26-gauge pink covered wire
18-gauge stem wire

1 Cut 45×80mm (1¹³⁄₁₆×3⅛in) rectangles of orange/pink silky ribbon, at least three for each flowerhead and one to make a bud. Cut out the petal shapes as shown and crinkle by the spiral twist method.

Tool the petal tips with the rose-petal curling head to curve them back slightly.

Cut 15mm (⁹⁄₁₆in) lengths of double-sided adhesive tape and cut them in half lengthwise. For each petal, lay a strip of double-sided tape along one side of the petal. Peel off the backing paper, pull round and attach the other edge of the petal to the tape to make a shallow cone.

2 To make a stamen centre, cut one 80mm (3⅛in) length of pink covered wire. Assemble seven stamens into a cluster and cut off the heads at one end. Arrange the stamens around the pink covered wire, with the cut ends 10mm (³⁄₈in) from the end of the wire. Fasten the stamens and wire with pink stem tape and curve the free ends gently outwards.

Drop the stamen centre into the petal cone with a short stem about 20mm (¹³⁄₁₆in) passing through the hole at the centre of the floret. Secure the base of the floret to the stamen centre by the twisting method, using 30-gauge wire. Trim the wires to about 25mm (1in) and cover with half-width green stem tape.

3 To make a bud, cut one petal into two sections. Roll the smaller piece and fasten it with 30-gauge wire by the twisting method. Leave an end of 30-gauge wire about 30mm (1³⁄₁₆in) long and tape it with half-width green stem tape.

Wrap the larger petal section around the bud with the petal tips curling inwards. Secure it with 30-gauge wire by the twisting method. Trim the wire to about 25mm (1in) length and neaten with half-width green stem tape.

Make three florets and one bud for a full flowerhead. Fasten them together at the base with half-width green stem tape and join in a short piece of 18-gauge uncovered wire.

4 Cut two 30×72mm (1³⁄₁₆×2¹³⁄₁₆in) rectangles of green silky ribbon; fold and cut each piece into four lengthwise. Lay a strip of double-sided adhesive tape down the centre of each of four rectangles. Cut four 60mm (2³⁄₈in) lengths of green covered wire. Attach a wire to the adhesive strip on each rectangle. Cover with the remaining pieces of green silky and cut the leaf shapes.

Mark leaf veins with scissor blades or with the tool blade head. Tape the leaf stems with half-width green stem tape.

Make enough leaves to clothe the flower stem and separate leaf stem as shown. Vary the leaf sizes, up to 20×48mm (¹³⁄₁₆×1⁷⁄₈in).

To assemble, tape the stem of the flowerhead with green stem tape, and attach leaves below the flowers on alternate sides of the stem.

To make the leaf stem, tape three small leaves to the tip of an 18-gauge wire, using half-width green stem tape. Work down the stem, adding leaves at intervals of about 10mm (³⁄₈in), fanning out around the stem and increasing in size.

Join the flower and leaf stems with green stem tape.

BELLS OF IRELAND (Moluccella)

MATERIALS
Silky ribbon in cream
Brown round stamens
Beige stem tape
5mm (³⁄₁₆in) double-sided adhesive tape
18-gauge stem wire

1 Cut sixteen squares of cream silky ribbon in each of four sizes: 24mm (¹⁵⁄₁₆in), 30mm (1³⁄₁₆in), 36mm (1⁷⁄₁₆in) and 42mm (1⁵⁄₈in).

Cut eight 48mm (1⁷⁄₈in) squares.

Cut a circle from each square by folding the square into four and cutting a curve across the corners as shown. Open out the circles and cut away a triangular segment in each.

Cut double-sided tape in half lengthwise and lay a narrow strip on one edge of the triangular cut in each circle. Gently stretch the ribbon just inside the edge of the circle all around. Remove the backing paper from the adhesive tape and stick the straight edges of the ribbon together to form each circle into a cone.

Cut the stamens in half to make seventy-two pieces. Tape each stamen stem with half-width beige stem tape.

Drop a stamen into each silky cone and secure at the base with stem tape.

Tape together three lengths of 18-gauge stem wire and cover with half-width stem tape. Tape the eight small bells in a cluster at the tip of this stem. Tape another cluster of eight bells about 20mm (¹³⁄₁₆in) below the first. Continue to attach the bells in groups of eight, gradually increasing in size. At the same time increase the distance between the clusters slightly, so that the final gap is 45mm (1¹³⁄₁₆in).

BIRD OF PARADISE (Strelitzia)

MATERIALS
Silky ribbon in deep pink, orange and deep blue
Acetate ribbon in green
Stem tape in orange and green
Double-sided adhesive tape in 36mm (1⁷⁄₁₆in) and 5mm (³⁄₁₆in) widths
30-gauge wire
24-gauge white covered wire
24-gauge green covered wire
16-gauge padded craft wire

1 Cut nine 36×100mm (1⁷⁄₁₆×3¹⁵⁄₁₆in) rectangles from orange silky ribbon and nine of the same dimensions in deep pink. Lay 36mm (1⁷⁄₁₆in) double-sided tape on each of the orange rectangles.

Cut nine 120mm (4³⁄₄in) lengths of white covered wire. Attach a length of wire down the centre of each rectangle. Place a deep pink rectangle over each of the orange rectangles and secure by pressing down onto the double-sided tape.

Cut each rectangle into the outline of petal A. Tool down the length of the petals with the ridged head. Alternatively, fold the petals lengthwise and crinkle by the spiral twist method.

17

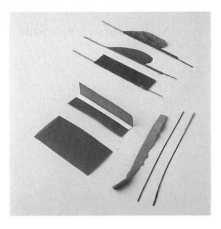

2 Cut three 36×72mm (1⁷⁄₁₆×2¹³⁄₁₆in) rectangles from blue silky ribbon. Fold them in half lengthwise and place a strip of 5mm (³⁄₁₆in) double-sided tape inside each fold as shown.

Cut three 120mm (4¾in) lengths of green covered wire. Thicken 30mm (1³⁄₁₆in) at one end of each wire with orange stem tape.

Attach a wire to the double-sided tape strip inside each blue rectangle, with the orange tip of the wire protruding at one end. Press down the ribbon along the fold and cut each rectangle into the outline of petal B. Tool with the ridged head as for petal A.

3 Cut one 48×130mm (1⁷⁄₈×5¹⁄₈in) rectangle from green acetate ribbon. Cut out the bract shape. Lay 5mm (³⁄₁₆in) double-sided adhesive tape along the centre and a small piece of tape along one side from the tip of the bract. Attach a length of green covered wire to the central strip of double-sided tape. Attach one petal A, orange side down, to the centre of the bract. Roll over the top edges of the bract and secure them by means of the adhesive tape at the top edge.

4 Place one petal B against the petal A inside the bract and position one petal A on either side. Fasten bract and petals at the base

by the twisting method using 30-gauge wire. Leave a wire stem of about 50mm (2in). Tape base and stem with half-width green stem tape.

5 Make up a second and third floret by grouping petals A and B in the same way as for the first but without including a bract.

Group the three florets together, with all the B petals facing away from the bract. Tape them together with full-width green stem tape and join in a length of 16-gauge padded craft wire.

Cut a 36×60mm (1⁷⁄₁₆×2³⁄₈in) rectangle of green acetate ribbon and cut out the shape of the small bract. Lay a short strip of 5mm (³⁄₁₆in) double-sided tape across the base of the bract on the matt side. Peel off the backing strip and attach the small bract to the flower stem below the florets, on the opposite side from the large bract.

To cover the stem, cut a strip of green acetate ribbon 24mm (¹⁵⁄₁₆in) wide and the same length as the length of stem required. Apply double-sided adhesive tape to the matt side and wrap the acetate ribbon around the stem, slightly overlapping the small bract.

If you are making several flower stems, it creates a good effect to add more florets to some of the flowerheads.

BLUEBELL (Endymion)

MATERIALS

Acetate ribbon in blue and green
Blue round stamens
Stem tape in blue and green
30-gauge wire
24-gauge green covered wire
20-gauge stem wire
36mm (1⁷⁄₁₆in) double-sided adhesive tape
Flowermaking adhesive

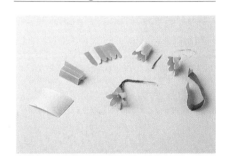

1 Cut a 24×36mm (¹⁵⁄₁₆×1⁷⁄₁₆in) rectangle from blue acetate ribbon. Fold it into six lengthwise and cut the fluted tips of the petals. Do not cut the ribbon down the length of the folds.

Curl back the petal tips by stroking outwards on the shiny side with closed scissor blades. Alternatively, tool the petal tips using the smooth curved head.

Roll the ribbon into a tube and stick the sides together with adhesive or with a very narrow strip of double-sided tape.

Cut one stamen string in half and tape the stamen stem with half-width blue stem tape to strengthen and slightly thicken it. Drop the stamen into the flower bell until the stamen tip sits just below the point where the petal tips curl outwards. Gather in the base of the flower and secure the stamen by the hairpin wiring method, using 30-gauge wire. Tape the base and about 15mm (9/16in) of wire with half-width green stem tape.

Repeat the process to make three more flower bells.

Cut a length of 20-gauge stem wire and tape one flower to the end of the wire. Continue taping down the stem and attach the other flowers at 20mm (13/16in) intervals on alternate sides of the stem but all facing in the same direction. Tape the remaining length of stem. Curve individual flower stems so that the bells hang downwards.

2 Cut two 72mm (2 13/16in) squares from green acetate ribbon. Apply double-sided tape to the matt side of one piece.

Cut four 50mm (2in) lengths of green covered wire and attach them to the adhesive tape at regular intervals, with 20mm (13/16in) of wire on the ribbon and the remainder forming a stem. Cover with the second square of ribbon and press down firmly.

Cut the green acetate ribbon into four leaf shapes, each with a central wire stem. Tape the leaves to the base of the flower stem.

BRIAR ROSE

MATERIALS

Shaded silky ribbon in white/pale pink
Silky ribbon in green
Brown-tipped yellow stamens
Ready-made rose leaves
Stem tape in yellow and green
30-gauge wire
28-gauge white covered wire
20-gauge stem wire
Flowermaking adhesive
Cotton wool

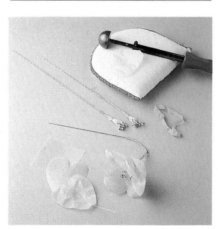

1 Cut five 60mm (2 3/8in) squares from shaded silky ribbon and shape the petals. Tool with the large mushroom head where indicated. Turn the petals over and tool the centres.

Turn each petal back and use adhesive to stick a length of white covered wire halfway up the petal, leaving an equal length as stem. Allow the adhesive to dry.

Thicken the top 20mm (13/16in) of a length of 20-gauge stem wire with yellow stem tape.

Put twenty stamen strings together and fold them in half. Arrange them around the thickened wire tip to make the flower centre. Secure with 30-gauge wire by the twisting method and bind with half-width yellow stem tape.

Arrange the petals around the flower centre to overlap sequentially. Secure with 30-gauge wire by the twisting method and neaten with yellow stem tape.

2 To make the bud, cut five 50mm (2in) squares of shaded silky ribbon and cut one petal shape from each square. Tool in the same way as for the large petal but using the small mushroom head.

Loop a length of 30-gauge wire around a piece of cotton wool, hold the wire and twist the cotton wool to secure it. Shape the cotton wool into a bud.

Using adhesive, stick one petal to the bud and fold the petal tips over the cotton wool to conceal it. Allow the adhesive to dry.

Stick on the remaining petals individually to build up the bud, curling back the tips of the petals. Secure the base of the bud with 30-gauge wire by the twisting method and neaten with half-width green stem tape.

3 Cut one 48mm (1 7/8in) square of green silky ribbon and one 36mm (1 7/16in) square. Fold each square by the five-point fold as shown and cut to make the calyces. Pierce a hole in the centre of each calyx using 20-gauge wire. Push the large calyx up the flower stem and secure underneath the flower with green stem tape. Repeat with the bud calyx.

Arrange the leaves in groups of three and tape to flower and bud stems. Tape flower and bud together and finish taping the stem.

BRONZE CHRYSANTHEMUM

MATERIALS
Two-colour silky ribbon in yellow/brown
Silky ribbon in green
Green stem tape
Ready-made chrysanthemum leaves
30-gauge wire
18-gauge stem wire
Flowermaking adhesive

1 From yellow/brown silky ribbon, cut one 36×72mm (1⁷⁄₁₆×2¹³⁄₁₆in) rectangle. Fold it into eight widthways and cut one flower centre.

Cut eight 72mm (2¹³⁄₁₆in) squares; fold and cut each one in the shape of petal A as shown.

Cut twelve squares in each of three sizes: 48mm (1⁷⁄₈in), 60mm (2³⁄₈in) and 72mm (2¹³⁄₁₆in). Fold and cut each in the shape of petal B as shown.

2 Tool each section of each petal from tip to base using the ridged head.

3 Tape the top 30mm (1³⁄₁₆in) of an 18-gauge stem wire. Use pliers to form a hook at the tip, hook it to one end of the flower centre and roll it up tightly. Secure with 30-gauge wire by the twisting method and neaten with green stem tape.

Make a small hole in the centre of each petal A. Push each one up the stem wire, put some adhesive inside and press each petal A to the base of the flower centre. Make sure the petals are as close as possible to the centre, concealing the stem tape.

Dab adhesive on the bottom of each of the small petals B and stick them evenly around the base of the flowerhead. Repeat with the medium-sized and large petals B.

4 Cut a 36mm (1⁷⁄₁₆in) square of green silky ribbon, fold and cut the calyx as shown. Make a hole in the centre and push the calyx up the flower stem under the base of the flower. Use adhesive to secure it in place and finish by taping.

Continue taping the flower stem, securing the leaves in position. Tape to finish the stem.

To make a smaller flower, omit the large petals B or alternatively both the medium and large sizes of petal B.

CAMELLIA

MATERIALS
Poplin ribbon in deep pink
Acetate ribbon in green
Velvet silky ribbon in white
Small piece of yellow ribbon
Small yellow stamens

Stem tape in white and green
30-gauge wire
24-gauge green covered wire
20-gauge stem wire
Double-sided adhesive tape in 5mm
(³⁄₁₆in) and 36mm (1⁷⁄₁₆in) widths
Flowermaking adhesive

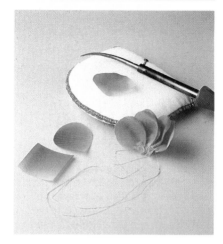

1 Cut five 48mm (1⁷⁄₈in) squares from pink poplin ribbon and cut petals. Stretch the centres of the petals to cup them slightly by pulling between thumbs and forefingers. Tool the top edges with the rose-petal curling head to curl them slightly.

Wire the five petals in single-row sequence using 30-gauge wire, with two twists of wire between one petal and the next.

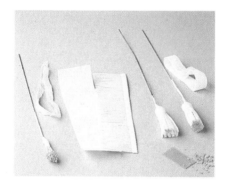

2 Assemble about thirty stamens, fold them in half and secure them with 30-gauge wire. Tape with half-width white stem tape and attach the stamen centre to a 20-gauge stem wire.

Cut a 36×130mm (1⁷⁄₁₆×5⅛in) rectangle of white velvet ribbon. Cut finely from one long edge to form a fringe and apply 5mm (³⁄₁₆in) double-sided adhesive tape to the bottom edge on the wrong side of the ribbon. Wrap the fringe around the stamen centre so that the tips of the stamens lie about 10mm (³⁄₈in) below the top of the fringe. Secure

with full-width white stem tape.
Apply a little adhesive to the top of the fringe. Cut the yellow ribbon into tiny pieces and dip the top of the fringed centre into them so they adhere to the fringe ends. Hold the fringed centre closed and press down slightly to curve it. Leave the centre until the adhesive is dry, then open it out slightly to reveal the stamens.

3 Wrap the wired petals around the flower centre. Join up the ends of 30-gauge wire, hold firmly and secure by twisting the flower. Neaten the flower base with green stem tape.

Cut four 36×50mm (1⁷⁄₁₆×2in) rectangles from green acetate ribbon. Apply 36mm (1⁷⁄₁₆in) double-sided tape to the matt sides of two of the rectangles.

Cut two 80mm (3⅛in) lengths of green covered wire. Attach a wire to the adhesive tape down the centre of each rectangle. Cover with a second rectangle of green acetate ribbon shiny side up. Cut out two leaves. Mark the leaf veins with scissor blades or the tool blade head.

Tape the end of a 20-gauge stem wire with green stem tape to form a node. Tape about 20mm (¹³⁄₁₆in) of each leaf stem with half-width green stem tape and join the leaves to the stem wire. Tape the leaf and flower stems together and finish taping the stem.

It creates a natural effect if you join a second pair of leaves to the flower stem so that the leaves stand above and below the flower.

Alternatively, use twig tape throughout and fasten flowers and leaves on to a real twig.

CARNATION
(Dianthus)

MATERIALS
Silky ribbon in pale yellow and grey/green
Stem tape in yellow and green
30-gauge wire
20-gauge stem wire

1 Cut nine 72mm (2¹³⁄₁₆in) squares of yellow silky ribbon. Fold and cut each square as shown to make the petals. Fringe the edges finely. Cut along one fold in each petal section to a little more than halfway down and refold concertina fashion.

Hold the base of a petal and dampen the thumb and forefinger of your free hand. Twist the petal sections alternately in different directions to stretch the outer edges. Treat all the petals in this way.

Secure the base of each petal by the twisting method using 30-gauge wire. Cut the ends of wire to different lengths but no less than 50mm (2in) long. Cover about 20mm ($^{13}/_{16}$in) of the wire with half-width yellow stem tape.

2 Cluster the wired petals together evenly to form the flowerhead. Secure them with half-width stem tape, making sure that each petal stands free. Join in a 20-gauge stem wire and secure it with green stem tape. Wrap green stem tape around the top of the stem wire close to the base of the flower.

Cut one 48×72mm ($1^7/_8$×$2^{13}/_{16}$in) rectangle of grey/green silky ribbon and fold concertina fashion at 6mm ($^1/_4$in) intervals. Cut the leaf shape as shown to make twelve leaves. Attach pairs of leaves to the flower stem by the twisting method using 30-gauge wire. Tape with half-width green stem tape to thicken the point where the leaves attach to the stem. Curl the leaves over closed scissor blades.

Thicken the end of a 20-gauge stem wire with green stem tape to form a bud. Join the bud to the flower stem and continue taping, adding further pairs of leaves at intervals down the stem. Tape to the end of the stem.

To make the spray carnation, make up smaller flowers by the same method using only five petals cut from 48mm ($1^7/_8$in) squares in each flowerhead. Join three small flowers and two buds to form the spray.

CHINESE LANTERN (Physalis Alkekengi)

MATERIALS

Two-colour silky ribbon in brown/ orange
Beige stem tape
28-gauge white covered wire
18-gauge stem wire
5mm ($^3/_{16}$in) double-sided adhesive tape

1 To make one lantern, cut five 28×72mm ($1^1/_8$×$2^{13}/_{16}$in) rectangles from two-colour silky ribbon and shape lantern sections, keeping the colour shading even in each piece. Fold each section in half lengthwise and crinkle by the spiral twist method.

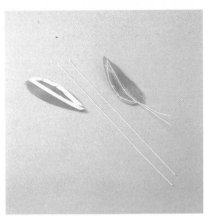

2 Place double-sided tape down the centre of each section, and down one side, working to the same side on each piece. Cut ten 150mm ($5^7/_8$in) lengths of white covered wire, two for each lantern section. Attach a wire to the adhesive tape down the centre and side of each section. Bend the outer wire to follow the shape and curve the centre wire gently.

3 Stick together the outer edges of the sections to form the five pieces into a lantern. Trim any uneven edges of ribbon. Cover the wires at the base with beige stem tape to form a stem. Hold the top and bottom of the lantern and apply gentle pressure to achieve the correct shape.

Make at least five lanterns for one stem. Attach the first lantern to the end of an 18-gauge stem wire and secure with half-width stem tape. Curve the lantern stem so the lantern points downwards. Continue taping down the main stem, adding each lantern singly.

A pleasing effect is achieved if the lanterns are made in progressively darker shades of the same colours, forming a colour gradation from light to dark down the stem.

CHRISTMAS ROSE
(Helleborus niger)

MATERIALS
Silky ribbon in white
Shaded silky ribbon in white/pale green
Acetate ribbon in green
Yellow pointed stamens
Stem tape in yellow and red/brown
30-gauge wire
28-gauge white covered wire
24-gauge green covered wire
20-gauge stem wire
Double-sided adhesive tape in 5mm (³⁄₁₆in) and 36mm (1⁷⁄₁₆in) widths

1 Cut five 48mm (1⁷⁄₈in) squares of white silky ribbon. Apply 5mm (³⁄₁₆in) double-sided tape diagonally across the centre of each square.

Cut a 24mm (1⁵⁄₁₆in) strip from the white side of the shaded ribbon, leaving a predominantly pale green section. Cut five 48mm (1⁷⁄₈in) squares of shaded ribbon.

Cut short lengths of white covered wire. Attach a wire to the adhesive tape across the centre of each white square, starting about 10mm (³⁄₈in) from the top. Cover with a square of shaded ribbon. Cut one petal on the diagonal of each square.

Stretch the petals just inside the edges and gently curve the wires to cup the petals slightly. The pale green colouring should be on the outside of each petal.

Wire the five petals in single-row sequence using 30-gauge wire. Leave an even allowance of 15mm (⁹⁄₁₆in) below the securing wire at the base of each petal.

2 Thicken the end of a 20-gauge stem wire with yellow stem tape.

Cut thirty-two stamen strings in half and divide the stamens into four bundles. Secure the base of each bundle with 30-gauge wire using the hairpin method. Position them evenly around the thickened stem end, with the base of the stamens just below the taped section and the stamen tips just above the stem end. Tape to hold them in place and secure with 30-gauge wire by the twisting method. Cover the wiring with tape.

Wrap the petals around the flower centre, keeping the concave curves in shape. The fifth petal should just overlap the first. Wind a long end of 30-gauge wire around the base of the petals and bring together all the ends of wire at the flower base. Twist the flowerhead to secure the wires and trim off the excess lengths.

3 Tape the base of the flower with red/brown stem tape and continue taping down the flower stem to the required length.

To make a smaller flower, cut five petal shapes from 36mm (1⁷⁄₁₆in) squares of silky ribbon. Line the petals and make up the flower as above.

To make a small bud, cut five petal shapes from 24mm (1⁵⁄₁₆in) squares of white silky ribbon. Do not line them but stretch them gently as for the larger petals. Wire the petals in single-row sequence. Make the bud centre by taping the end of a stem wire to form a small node but do not attach stamens. Wrap the petals around the node and secure as for the full size flower.

Cut two 60×100mm (2³⁄₈×3¹⁵⁄₁₆in) rectangles of green acetate ribbon. Apply 36mm (1⁷⁄₁₆in) double-sided tape to one of these rectangles on the matt side of the ribbon.

Cut five 100mm (3¹⁵⁄₁₆in) lengths of green covered wire. Attach them to the adhesive tape, evenly spaced across the width of the rectangle and starting about 10mm (³⁄₈in) from the top edge.

Place the second rectangle of green acetate ribbon over the first, shiny side up and press down firmly. Divide the strip into five equal sections and cut a leaf from each one. Tape the leaf stems together to make a fan of leaves.

Using red/brown stem tape, attach the smaller flower and bud to the main flower stem and join in the leaves below the flowers.

CLEMATIS MONTANA

blade head. Colour the edges with the red felt-tip pen. Tape the three leaves together in a trefoil grouping.

Repeat to make two more leaf groups.

To assemble, tape flowers and leaves to an 18-gauge stem wire and cover the wire with red brown stem tape. This clematis flowers profusely, so if you are making a large stem or full plant, it may be necessary to tape together several wires to provide support. A natural effect is achieved by varying the leaf sizes if several groupings are made.

CLIVIA

MATERIALS
Silky ribbon in pale pink and green
Yellow heavy cotton thread
Green embroidery silk
Stem tape in green and red brown
30-gauge wire
30-gauge green covered wire
30-gauge white covered wire
18-gauge stem wire
5mm (³⁄₁₆in) double-sided adhesive tape
Red felt-tip pen

1 Cut four 36mm (1⁷⁄₁₆in) squares of pink silky ribbon. Fold each square in half, crease the fold and open out the square.

Apply double-sided tape down the centre of one half of each square. Attach one 70mm (2³⁄₄in) length of 30-gauge white covered wire to each piece of tape. Fold over the other half of the square and press down firmly. Cut one petal from each rectangle.

Tool the petals down either side of the wire with the ridged head. If the tip of the petal looks square, trim to round it.

2 Cut a 70mm (2³⁄₄in) length of green embroidery silk and loop it around one finger. Wrap a length of yellow cotton thread three times around your finger to cover the green loop. Slip the combined threads off your finger and hook a short length of 30-gauge wire through the loops. Twist the wire to secure. Twist a small piece of 30-gauge wire around the threads just above the first wire. Cut the top of the looped thread to make a silky tassel. Spread the tassel and trim the green threads to short lengths. Neaten the base of the tassel with green stem tape.

Arrange the petals around the tassel centre, tooled side inwards, and secure with half-width red-brown stem tape.

Repeat to make a second flower.

3 Cut three 65×72mm (2⁹⁄₁₆×2¹³⁄₁₆in) rectangles of green silky ribbon. Fold in half widthways and place a strip of double-sided tape down the centre of one half of each rectangle. Attach a length of 30-gauge green covered wire to each piece of adhesive tape. Fold over the other half of the rectangle to line the first.

Cut the leaves and mark the leaf veins with scissor blades or the tool

MATERIALS
Shaded silky ribbon in orange/white
Acetate ribbon in green
Yellow round stamens
Green stem tape
30-gauge white covered wire
28- and 24-gauge green covered wire
18-gauge stem wire
16-gauge padded craft wire
Double-sided adhesive tape in 5mm (³⁄₁₆in) and 36mm (1⁷⁄₁₆in) widths

1 Cut twelve 24×72mm (¹⁵⁄₁₆×2¹³⁄₁₆in) rectangles of shaded silky ribbon. Lay a strip of

double-sided tape across the centre of each of six rectangles.

Cut six 80mm (3⅛in) lengths of white covered wire. Attach a wire to the adhesive tape down the centre of each rectangle, starting about 20mm (¹³⁄₁₆in) from the top.

Place a second rectangle of ribbon over the first and press down firmly.

Cut one petal shape from each rectangle, keeping the orange edge of the ribbon to the top of the petal. Tool around the top edges of the petals with the small ball head to stretch the ribbon. Gently curve the reinforcing wires.

Gather a small bundle of yellow stamens and cut off the heads at one end. Secure the cut ends with 30-gauge wire by the twisting method. Tape the base of the stamen centre with half-width green stem tape.

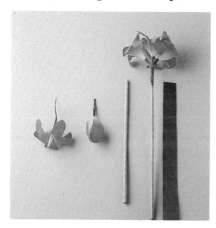

2 Place three petals around the stamen centre and secure with half-width green stem tape. Place another three petals over the spaces between the first three and secure with tape, continuing to tape about 20mm (¹³⁄₁₆in) down the stem. Make sure all the petals are curving outwards.

To make a bud, cut and line three petals and tape them around the stamen centre with the petals curving inwards.

For a full flowerhead, make a total of five flowers and two buds.

Tape flowers and buds together in a radiating cluster, using full-width green stem tape. Allow a short stem on each flower so that the flowerhead can be opened out to a pleasing shape.

Bind a length of 16-gauge padded craft wire to the flower stem using full-width green stem tape. Cut a 24×300mm (¹⁵⁄₁₆×11⅞in) piece of green acetate ribbon and apply double-sided tape to the matt side of

the ribbon. Peel the backing paper from the double-sided tape and wrap the acetate strip around the padded stem.

3 Cut ten 9×24mm (⁵⁄₁₆×¹⁵⁄₁₆in) rectangles of green acetate ribbon. On five rectangles, lay two strips of 5mm (³⁄₁₆in) double-sided tape on the wrong side of the ribbon.

Cut five 25mm (1in) lengths of 28-gauge green covered wire. Attach a wire to the adhesive tape down the centre of each rectangle. Cover with a second rectangle of acetate ribbon shiny side up. Cut the sepal shapes.

Bend each sepal back at right angles to its stem. Position them evenly spaced around the base of the flowerhead and secure with green stem tape.

Cut two 36×100mm (1⁷⁄₁₆×3¹⁵⁄₁₆in) rectangles of green acetate ribbon. Apply 36mm (1⁷⁄₁₆in) double-sided tape to the matt side of one rectangle. Cut a 120mm (4¾in) length of 24-gauge green covered wire. Attach the wire to the adhesive tape down the centre of the rectangle, starting about 10mm (⅜in) from the top. Press the second rectangle of ribbon over the first. Cut the leaf shape.

Make several leaves, varying the sizes, to be taped to the base of the flower stem.

MATERIALS
Silky ribbon in purple, yellow and green
Yellow stamens
Stem tape in light green and dark green
28-gauge green covered wire
5mm (³⁄₁₆in) double-sided adhesive tape
Flowermaking adhesive

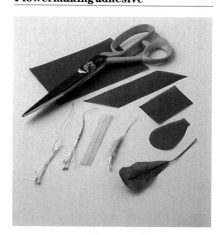

1 Cut six petals across the grain of the purple ribbon, as shown. Dampen your fingers and stretch each petal along its length.

Cut six 110mm (4⁵⁄₁₆in) lengths of green covered wire and use adhesive to attach a wire down the centre of each petal.

Cut a 10×72mm (⅜×2¹³⁄₁₆in) rectangle of yellow silky ribbon. Apply double-sided tape along one long edge of the ribbon. Fringe the other edge finely down to the line of the tape.

Assemble five yellow stamens and cut off the heads at one end. Adjust the stamens so that the heads are at different heights and secure the base with 30-gauge wire and light green stem tape.

Remove the backing paper from the double-sided tape on the fringe and wind the fringe in a spiral down the length of the stamens, starting just below the stamen heads. Tape the base with half-width light green stem tape.

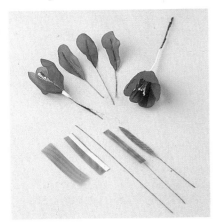

2 Position three petals around the flower centre and secure with half-width light green stem tape. Put the other three petals over the spaces between the first three and tape in place.

To make one leaf, cut one 15×60mm (9/16×2⅜in) rectangle of green silky ribbon. Apply double-sided tape to half of the rectangle lengthwise. Cut a 120mm (4¾in) length of green covered wire. Attach the wire down the centre of the adhesive tape. Fold over and press down the other half of the rectangle. Cut the leaf shape.

Make four or five leaves to one flower, varying the sizes if preferred. Tape the leaves to the flower stem with half-width dark green stem tape.

CYCLAMEN

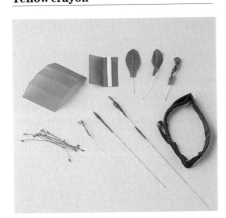

MATERIALS

Silky ribbon in cyclamen pink and green
Velvet silky ribbon in green
Pink stamens
Red-brown stem tape
30-gauge wire
28-gauge white covered wire
24-gauge green covered wire
20-gauge stem wire
Double-sided adhesive tape in 5mm (3/16in) and 24mm (15/16in) widths
Yellow crayon

1 Cut a 36×50mm (1⁷⁄₁₆×2in) rectangle of pink silky ribbon and fold it in half lengthwise. Apply a strip of double-sided tape down the centre of one half. Cut an 80mm (3⅛in) length of white covered wire. Attach the wire to the adhesive tape. Fold over the other half of the ribbon and press down firmly.

Make five petals for the flower and three for the bud. Crinkle by the spiral twist method.

Fold two stamens in half and secure the base with 30-gauge wire. Tape the base with half-width stem tape.

Cut a stem-length of 20-gauge wire and position the stamen centre at the top, with the stamen heads just above the end of the wire. Secure the stamens with stem tape and continue taping to thicken the stem end.

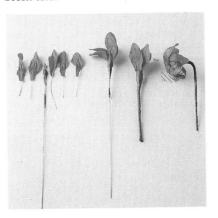

2 Assemble the five petals around the flower centre, overlapping each other slightly, and tape them in place. Thicken the length of the stem below the flowerhead with stem tape.

Turn back the flower petals to show the flower full face. Bend the stem about 25mm (1in) below the base of the flower.

3 To make the bud, thicken the end of a length of 20-gauge stem wire. Position three petals around the thickened stem end and secure with stem tape. Thicken the full stem and bend it below the bud as for the flower.

To make the closed bud, thicken the end of a length of stem wire to form a pointed bud shape. Thicken and bend the stem as before.

4 Cut one 45mm (1¹³⁄₁₆in) square of green velvet ribbon and one of green silky ribbon. Apply double-sided tape to the wrong side of the velvet ribbon square. Position a length of 24-gauge green covered wire down the centre of the square and cover with the silky ribbon square.

Cut the leaf shape and apply the leaf markings using the yellow crayon. Mark the leaf veins with scissor blades or the tool blade head. Tape the leaf stem with red-brown stem tape.

Make second and third size leaves from 36mm (1⁷⁄₁₆in) and 30mm (1³⁄₁₆in) squares respectively.

Arrange the flower, buds and leaves in a neat grouping and secure the stems with tape.

DAFFODIL (Narcissus)

MATERIALS

Silky ribbon in yellow, cream, brown and green
Yellow stamens
Stem tape in yellow and green
30-gauge wire
28- and 24-gauge white covered wire
24-gauge green covered wire
20-gauge stem wire
5mm (³⁄₁₆in) double-sided adhesive tape
Flowermaking adhesive
Orange felt-tip pen

1 To make the yellow trumpet, cut one 60mm (2³⁄₈in) square of yellow silky ribbon and cut trumpet A as shown. Crinkle by the damp cloth method and stretch the outer edge between thumb and forefinger.

Cut a 45mm (1¹³⁄₁₆in) length of double-sided tape and halve it lengthwise. Run a narrow strip along one straight edge of the trumpet shape. Remove the backing paper from the tape and attach a piece of 24-gauge white covered wire along two-thirds of the straight edge. Bring the two straight edges of the shape together to form the trumpet and secure them with the adhesive tape.

Tool the top edge of the trumpet with the rose-petal curling tool to curl it back slightly.

Cover 70mm (2¾in) of a 20-gauge stem wire with yellow stem tape. Continue taping to thicken the top of the stem into a flower centre. Place the trumpet on the stem wire and secure it around the centre by the twisting method, using 30-gauge wire. Cover the trumpet base with green stem tape.

To make the orange-edged trumpet, cut the fan shape for trumpet B from a 50×72mm (2×2¹³⁄₁₆in) rectangle of yellow silky ribbon. Crinkle by the damp cloth method and stretch the outer curve between thumb and forefinger. Form the trumpet shape as above. Tool the top edge of the trumpet to curl it and colour it with the orange felt-tip pen.

Assemble a small bundle of yellow stamens and cut off the heads at one end. Pull one stamen up slightly and secure the others around it with yellow stem tape. Tape the stamens to a 20-gauge stem wire. Place the orange-edged trumpet on the stem wire and secure it as above.

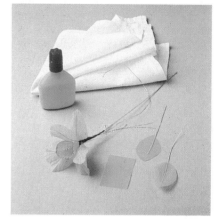

2 Cut six 36×60mm (1⁷⁄₁₆×2³⁄₈in) rectangles of cream silky ribbon and shape petals. Crinkle by the damp cloth method. Use adhesive to stick a length of 28-gauge white covered wire down the centre of each petal.

Wire the petals together in double-row sequence using 30-gauge wire, with the petal stem wires all facing away from you.

Wrap the petals around the orange-edged trumpet with the petal stem wires on the outside of the flower. Wind the long ends of the 30-gauge wire around the flower base. Hold all the wires together and twist the flowerhead to secure. Cover with green stem tape. Tape down about 40mm (1⁹⁄₁₆in) of the flower stem.

Follow the same process to make six petals from yellow silky ribbon and secure them around the yellow trumpet.

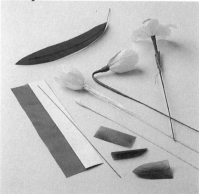

3 Cut a 24×45mm (¹⁵⁄₁₆×1¹³⁄₁₆in) rectangle of brown silky ribbon and shape the bract. Crinkle by the

damp cloth method. Attach the bract to the flower stem at the bottom of the taped section by the twisting method, using 30-gauge wire. Cover the base of the bract with green stem tape and continue taping down the stem. Bend the flower stem where the bract joins.

To make a bud, make six petals reinforced with wire as for the flower and wire them in double-row sequence. Thicken the end of a 20-gauge stem wire with yellow stem tape and wrap the petals around it with the reinforcing wires on the inside. Secure them in the same way as the flower petals and neaten with green stem tape. Apply a bract at the base of the bud, overlapping the petals. Bend the stem about 30mm (1³⁄₁₆in) below the bud base.

Cut a 48×200mm (1⁷⁄₈×7⁷⁄₈in) rectangle of green silky ribbon and apply a strip of double-sided tape to one half of the rectangle lengthwise. Attach a length of 24-gauge green covered wire down the centre of the taped half. Fold over the other half of the rectangle to line the first fully. Cut the leaf shape. Make at least two leaves and, if more, vary the sizes, keeping the long, narrow proportions.

EASTER LILY (Lilium longiflorum)

MATERIALS
Acetate ribbon in white and green
Large lily stamens
Stem tape in white, pale green and mid green

26-gauge white covered wire
24-gauge green covered wire
18-gauge stem wire
Double-sided adhesive tape in 5mm (³⁄₁₆in) and 36mm (1⁷⁄₁₆in) widths
Yellow felt-tip pen

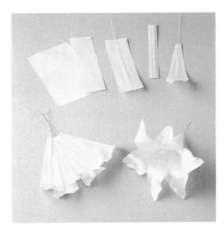

1 Cut nine 36×120mm (1⁷⁄₁₆×4³⁄₄in) rectangles of white acetate ribbon. Cut nine narrow strips of white acetate ribbon and attach 5mm (³⁄₁₆in) double-sided tape to each strip on the shiny side. Strip line the centre of each rectangle, inserting a length of white covered wire under each lining strip. Cut the petal shapes and stretch them between thumb and forefinger on either side of the petal tip.

To make the flower, place strips of 5mm (³⁄₁₆in) double-sided tape on both long side edges of three of the petals. Peel the backing paper from the tape and join six petals together, alternating one taped petal and one untaped. Join the petals into a trumpet, keeping the wires on the outside.

2 Colour the tips of six stamens with the yellow felt-tip pen. Tape down each stamen stem with half-width white stem tape to strengthen.

To make the pistil for the flower centre, cut three 120mm (4³⁄₄in) lengths of white covered wire. Bend them over to make loops and cover with white stem tape. Join in a 120mm (4³⁄₄in) length of white wire and tape all the wires together with half-width white stem tape.

Assemble the six stamens with the pistil in the centre, standing 10mm (³⁄₈in) above the stamens. Attach this stamen centre to a length of 18-gauge wire and thicken with pale green stem tape. Insert the flower centre into the throat of the flower.

Cover the base of the flower with green stem tape and continue taping down the flower stem.

3 To make the bud, join the remaining three petals as for the flower, keeping the reinforcing wires on the inside.

Thicken the end of an 18-gauge stem wire with yellow stem tape and tape down 100mm (3¹⁵⁄₁₆in) of the wire. Insert the wire into the bud, with the thickened end forming the bud centre. Secure the bud base with green stem tape and tape down the stem.

Cut a 36×72mm (1⁷⁄₁₆×2¹³⁄₁₆in) rectangle of green acetate ribbon. Fold it in half lengthwise and apply double-sided tape to one half of the rectangle on the matt side of the ribbon. Attach a length of green covered wire down the centre of the taped half. Fold over the other half of the rectangle and smooth it down. Cut out the leaf.

Make four more leaves and tape them singly to the bud and flower stems at intervals.

FORSYTHIA

MATERIALS
Silky ribbon in yellow
Yellow stamens
Brown stem tape
20-gauge stem wire
Flowermaking adhesive

1 To make one floret, cut a 36mm (1⁷⁄₁₆in) square of yellow silky ribbon, fold it in four and cut the petal shape as shown.

Open out the shape and tool around the floret with the small ball head, letting it curl naturally. Make a hole at the centre of the floret with a darning needle.

Cut one head off a stamen string. Apply adhesive to the string at least 5mm (³⁄₁₆in) below the remaining stamen head. Push the stamen through the centre of the floret until the head stands 5mm (³⁄₁₆in) above the centre. Allow the adhesive to dry.

Make at least ten florets for each main flower stem.

2 Thicken the end of a 20-gauge stem wire with half-width brown stem tape to form a node. Attach the flowers to the stem with half-width brown stem tape, two or three clustered together at intervals. Finish taping the stem.

To make a spray, tape individual stems together in a natural branching effect.

FREESIA

MATERIALS
Silky ribbon in cream and green
Yellow stamens
Green stem tape
30-gauge wire
20-gauge stem wire
5mm (³⁄₁₆in) double-sided adhesive tape
Flowermaking adhesive

1 Cut a 48×96mm (1⁷⁄₈×3¹³⁄₁₆in) rectangle of cream silky ribbon. Fold it in half to make a square. Fold into three from one corner, as shown, and cut the petal shape. Open out the petal and cut in half to make two petal sections. Tool each section with the small ball head to curl the petal tips.

2 Put a spot of adhesive into the centre of one petal section. Place the second section on top so that its points lie between those of the first, with all petal tips curling away from you. While the petal is still damp with adhesive, cup it with your fingers. Allow to dry.

Stick the edges of the petals together to form them into a trumpet. Use the covered head of a ballpoint pen to work it into the shape.

Make at least five flowers for each stem.

To make a bud, stick two petal sections together with the inner petals curling inwards and the outer petals outwards, or with both rings of petals curling inwards.

3 Cut a 20×24mm (¹³⁄₁₆×¹⁵⁄₁₆in) rectangle of green silky ribbon and fold into three widthways, with

one side behind the central section and one in front. Cut a point at top and bottom and tool the folded ribbon with the smooth curved head. Cut on the folds to form the calyx shapes.

Make two calyces for each flower.

4 Assemble three stamens and cut off the heads at one end. Insert the stamens into the centre of the flower so the heads are in line with the level at which the petals open out.

Hold the base of the flower carefully, put the calyces in place and secure the base of the flower by the twisting method, using 30-gauge wire. Cover with half-width green stem tape and tape down the stem about 15mm (9/16in).

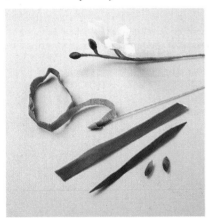

5 Thicken the top 10mm (3/8in) of a 20-gauge stem wire with green stem tape to form a node. Attach

two calyces by the twisting method, using 30-gauge wire, and tape a short distance down the stem wire. Join in a second node and continue taping down the stem with half-width green stem tape, positioning the buds and flowers at intervals.

Cut a 10×100mm (3/8×3 15/16in) strip of green silky ribbon and fold it in half lengthwise. Apply double-sided tape down the length on one side. Peel the backing paper from the tape and fold the other side of the rectangle over to line the first. Cut points at either end of the leaf.

Make two or three leaves and attach them to the bottom of the flower stem. Varying the leaf sizes creates a natural effect.

FUCHSIA

MATERIALS

Silky ribbon in pink and mauve
Acetate ribbon in green
Deep pink stamens
Stem tape in deep pink and green
30-gauge wire
28-gauge white covered wire
28-gauge green covered wire
20-gauge stem wire
36mm (1 7/16in) double-sided adhesive tape

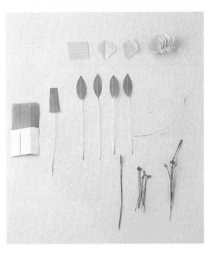

1 To make the inner petals, cut six 30mm (1 3/16in) squares of mauve silky ribbon. Cut the petal shape on the cross in each square, as shown. Crinkle by the damp cloth method and cup with your fingers while still damp.

Wire the petals in single-row sequence using 30-gauge wire, twisting the wire twice between the first and second petals.

To make the outer petals, cut one 36×72mm (1 7/16×2 13/16in) rectangle of deep pink silky ribbon. Fold in half to form a square. Cover one half with double-sided adhesive tape, then fold lengthwise into three rectangles. Attach a length of white covered wire down the centre of each taped section. Fold the remaining ribbon over the taped section to line it. Cut into three and cut out the petal shapes.

Make four fully lined petals for each flower.

Thicken the end of a length of white covered wire with deep pink stem tape and continue taping down 70mm (2 3/4in) of the wire.

Assemble nine stamens and cut off the heads at one end. Position them around the taped wire and secure by the twisting method, using 30-gauge wire. Neaten with stem tape.

2 Position the first two inner petals around the stamen centre to face each other. Wind the remaining petals around them. Hold the wires together and twist the flowerhead to secure. Cover the base with deep pink stem tape.

Arrange the four outer petals around the inner ring and secure with deep pink stem tape. Thicken the base of the flower with tape. Tape 40mm (1 9/16in) of the main stem with green stem tape.

To make a bud, thicken the end of a 20-gauge wire with deep pink stem tape to form a node. Make the bud quite large. Cover the stem below the bud with green stem tape.

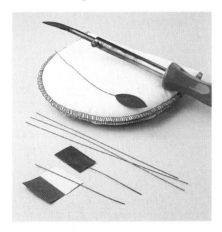

3 Cut a 36×40mm (1⁷⁄₁₆×1⁹⁄₁₆in) rectangle of green acetate ribbon and fold it in half lengthwise. Cover one half with double-sided tape. Attach a length of green covered wire to the centre of the taped rectangle. Fold over the remaining half of the rectangle to line the first.

Cut out the leaf shape and mark the veins using scissor blades or the tool blade head. Make at least four leaves per flower stem.

Assemble the flower, bud and leaves and tape together to form a single stem.

GERANIUM

MATERIALS

Silky ribbon in pale pink and green
Printed geranium leaves
Stem tape in pink and green
26-gauge green covered wire
26-gauge white covered wire
18-gauge stem wire
Double-sided adhesive tape in 5mm (³⁄₁₆in) and 36mm (1⁷⁄₁₆in) widths

1 Cut twenty-five 18×26mm (¹¹⁄₁₆×1¹⁄₁₆in) rectangles from pale pink silky ribbon and shape petals. Group them in fives. Tool the petal tips around the curves with the small ball head. Turn over the petals and apply a small piece of 5mm (³⁄₁₆in) double-sided tape to the base of each.

Cut two 70mm (2¾in) lengths of white covered wire and thicken the tips with half-width pink stem tape. Keeping the tips apart, tape the wires together about 10mm (³⁄₈in) below the tips.

Remove the backing paper from the double-sided tape on five petal bases. Press one petal firmly against the stamen centre, securing with the adhesive tape. Apply four more petals, singly, so that each partly overlaps the one before. Press them

firmly on to the flower centre and tape the stem with half-width green stem tape.

Make up four more florets in the same way.

2 To make a bud, cut a short length of white covered wire and thicken the tip to form a node. Tape the bud stem with half-width green stem tape.

Assemble a cluster of florets and buds and tape the stem bases together with half-width green stem tape.

3 Cut around the outline of a printed geranium leaf. Lay a piece of 36mm (1⁷⁄₁₆in) double-sided tape on the back. Cut one 100mm (3¹⁵⁄₁₆in) length of green covered wire and four 20mm (¹³⁄₁₆in) lengths.

Attach the long section of wire to the double-sided tape down the centre of the leaf, starting about 5mm (³⁄₁₆in) from the top. Position the four short wires radiating from the leaf centre. Cover with a rectangle of green silky ribbon cut to the full size of the leaf. Press it down firmly and trim the edges around the leaf outline.

Tape about 30mm (1³⁄₁₆in) of the leaf stem with half-width green stem tape. Tool the main leaf veins with the blade head.

Make several leaves and assemble them around the cluster of florets. Tape the main stem to finish. Alternatively, use green flocked ribbon to make leaves.

GLADIOLUS

MATERIALS
Silky ribbon in white and light green
Large yellow lily stamens
Stem tape in light green and white
30-gauge wire
28-gauge white covered wire
18-gauge stem wire
Flowermaking adhesive

1 Cut fifteen 36×70mm (1⁷⁄₁₆×2³⁄₄in) rectangles and nine 48×90mm (1⁷⁄₈×3⁹⁄₁₆in) rectangles from white silky ribbon and shape small and large petals. Crinkle using the damp cloth method.

Cut twenty-four 90mm (3⁹⁄₁₆in) lengths of white covered wire. Using flowermaking adhesive, stick a length of wire down the centre of each petal, starting about 10mm (³⁄₈in) from the tip. Gently stretch the petals around the upper curves.

Strengthen the stems of three large lily stamens with half-width white stem tape. Cut three 120mm (4³⁄₄in) lengths of white covered wire and bend each one into a right angle 10mm (³⁄₈in) below the tip.

Tape the three wires together with half-width white stem tape about 20mm (1³⁄₁₆in) below the angles. Assemble the three lily stamens around the wires and tape all together 65mm (2⁹⁄₁₆in) from the top.

Make two more stamen centres.

2 Arrange three small petals around the stamen centre and secure them with half-width white stem tape. Arrange three large petals around them to cover the spaces between the first three, keeping the right side of the ribbon inwards. Tape them in place with half-width green stem tape. Gently curve the petals outwards to show the stamens.

Join in an 18-gauge stem wire and secure with green stem tape.

Make two more flowers in the same way.

To make a bud, tape three small petals together and curve them inwards to make a closed shape. Join in an 18-gauge stem wire and cover with green stem tape. Make a second bud in the same way.

3 To make two bracts, cut a 72×90mm (2¹³⁄₁₆×3⁹⁄₁₆in) rectangle of green silky ribbon. Fold in half diagonally and cut along the fold to make two triangles. Cut one bract from each as shown.

For a full flower stem, cut twelve bracts in all. Crinkle by the damp cloth method and leave two bracts closed after crinkling.

Wire the two closed bracts together, one slightly higher than the other, by the twisting method using 30-gauge wire. Tape the base with half-width green stem tape. Join in two lengths of 18-gauge stem wire and tape. Wrap another bract around the stem, slightly overlapping the top two. Secure in the same way with wire and tape. Add another bract on the opposite side of the stem.

Tape one bud to the stem and wrap a bract around the stem partly enclosing the bud. Continue to work down the stem, adding a second bud with bract, then a flower and bract, securing them all in the same way. Alternate them on each side of the stem. Finish taping the full stem.

When making a very long stem, add larger flowers at the lower end. Cut the small petals from 36×80mm (1⁷⁄₁₆×3¹⁄₈in) and the large from 60×100mm (2³⁄₈×3¹⁵⁄₁₆in) rectangles of white silky ribbon.

HYACINTH

MATERIALS
Acetate ribbon in purple and green
Stem tape in green and yellow
30-gauge wire
24-gauge green covered wire
20-gauge stem wire
36mm (1⁷⁄₁₆in) double-sided adhesive tape

1 Cut thirty-six 48mm (1⅞in) squares of blue acetate ribbon and fold as shown. Cut one floret from each square. Tool the petal tips on the matt side of the ribbon using the smooth curved head, working from tip to centre on each section of the petal. On the shiny side of the ribbon, cup the petal base using the mushroom head.

Tape a 50mm (2in) length of 20-gauge wire with half-width yellow stem tape to make a pistil. Wrap the floret, shiny side inwards, around the pistil, bringing the side edges together. The tip of the pistil sits inside the floret. Secure by the twisting method using 30-gauge wire and tape down 25mm (1in) of the stem with half-width green stem tape.

Complete thirty-six florets to make one flowerhead.

2 Bind together three 20-gauge stem wires with green stem tape to form the main stem.

Bend each floret stem at an angle of about 60 degrees below the floret base. Position four florets at the top of the main stem, pointing outwards and upwards. Secure with green stem tape. Continue to add florets in groups of four about 15mm (9/16in) apart. Tape to the end of the stem.

Cut two 64×80mm (2½×3⅛in) rectangles of green acetate ribbon. Fold in half lengthwise with the shiny side out, open out the fold and

cover one side of each rectangle wth double-sided tape. Attach a length of 24-gauge green covered wire down the centre of each taped section. Fold over the other side of the rectangle to line the first. Cut the leaf shapes.

Attach the leaves to the base of the stem by the twisting method and tape to finish.

If adding a cluster of leaves, vary the sizes up to 160mm (6⁵/16in) in length.

HYDRANGEA

MATERIALS
Two-colour silky ribbon in wine red/pink
Acetate ribbon in dark green
Silky ribbon in dark green
Pink round stamens
Green stem tape
24-gauge green covered wire
18-gauge stem wire
36mm (1⁷/16in) double-sided adhesive tape
Flowermaking adhesive

1 To make one floret, cut a 36mm (1⁷/16in) square of two-colour silky ribbon, fold it in four and cut the petal shape as shown.

Open out the folds and tool from each corner into the centre using the small ball head. Turn over the floret and tool the centre. Make a small hole at the centre.

Cut off the head at one end of a stamen string. Put a spot of glue around the hole at the centre of the floret and insert the stamen so that the remaining head sits in the floret centre.

Repeat to make thirty-six florets in all. Cut some florets from the plain edge of the ribbon and some on the shaded section to vary the colour.

2 Assemble four florets on a length of green covered wire and tape in place with green stem tape.

Make nine groups of florets for one flowerhead. Assemble them around an 18-gauge stem wire with each group of florets standing out at least 40mm (1⁹/16in) from the main stem. Secure with green stem tape.

3 Cut a 50×72mm (2×2¹³/16in) rectangle of green acetate ribbon and one the same size of green silky. Cover the matt side of the acetate with double-sided tape. Attach a length of green covered wire down the centre and cover with the rectangle of green silky ribbon. Cut the leaf shape as shown.

Mark the leaf veins with scissor blades or the tool blade head. Tape the stem with half-width green stem tape.

Make enough leaves to attach pairs down the main flower stem at intervals, varying the sizes if there are several pairs. Tape to the end of the stem.

IRIS

MATERIALS
Silky ribbon in blue, yellow and green
Acetate ribbon in green
Green stem tape
30-gauge white covered wire
26-gauge blue covered wire
24-gauge green covered wire
18-gauge stem wire
Double-sided adhesive tape in 5mm (^{3}⁄$_{16}$in) and 24mm (^{15}⁄$_{16}$in) widths
Flowermaking adhesive
Tissue paper

1 From blue silky ribbon, cut three 72mm (2^{13}⁄$_{16}$in) squares and shape petals A, cut three 36×72mm

(1^7⁄$_{16}$×2^{13}⁄$_{16}$in) rectangles and shape petals B and cut six 36×72mm (1^7⁄$_{16}$×2^{13}⁄$_{16}$in) rectangles and shape petals C.

Cover a length of white covered wire with double-sided tape and curve it right around the edge of one petal A. Roll the edge of the petal over the wire. Do the same with the other two petals A. Crinkle by the damp cloth method.

Cut three 10×50mm (^{3}⁄$_8$×2in) rectangles of yellow silky ribbon. Place a strip of double-sided tape down the centre of each and cut the tongue of the flower as shown. Attach a tongue 36mm (1^7⁄$_{16}$in) from the tip of petal A.

Crinkle all other petals by the damp cloth method. Stick reinforcing wires to the centre of each, using blue covered wire and flowermaking adhesive.

Place a 36mm (1^7⁄$_{16}$in) length of double-sided tape at the base of each petal B on the opposite side to the wire. Remove the backing paper from the tape and attach a petal B to each petal A. Bend petal B back to show the flower tongue.

2 Tape together two lengths of 18-gauge wire with green stem tape. Thicken about 20mm (1^3⁄$_{16}$in) at the top of the stem with green stem tape.

Position the combined petals around the top of the wire with each petal A turning downwards. Secure with green stem tape.

Position three petals C, with the reinforcing wires on the inside, to sit curving upwards in the spaces between the combined petals. Secure with green stem tape. Tape to the bottom of the flower stem, thicken the full length with tissue paper and then tape again.

3 To make a bud, tape two lengths of 18-gauge wire together and thicken about 20mm (^{13}⁄$_{16}$in) at the top with green stem tape. Place the remaining three petals C around the top of the stem to form a closed bud and secure with green stem tape. Tape and thicken the stem as for the flower.

Cut four 24×100mm (^{15}⁄$_{16}$×3^{15}⁄$_{16}$in) rectangles of green silky ribbon and four the same size of green acetate ribbon.

Cover each silky rectangle with 24mm (^{15}⁄$_{16}$in) double-sided tape and reinforce with green covered wire. Line them with the acetate ribbon rectangles, matt side upwards. Cut a bract shape from each one.

Wrap two bracts around the bud stem, one slightly below the other partially covering the bud. Secure by the twisting method and cover the bract bases with green stem tape. Apply the other two bracts to the flower stem below the flower base.

4 Make a leaf in the same way as the bract but increase the length and use 20-gauge wire covered with half-width green stem tape as reinforcement. Tape the leaf to the flower stem.

LARGE ROSE

Wire three petals in single-row sequence, with the concave surface of the cupping facing you. Wrap these around the petal centre and fasten the ends with 30-gauge wire, taking the long lengths right around the flower base to join with the short ends. Twist the flower to secure. Trim the wires and neaten with half-width stem tape.

Wire eight petals in double-row sequence and wrap these around the inner petals. Secure as above and tape the flower base.

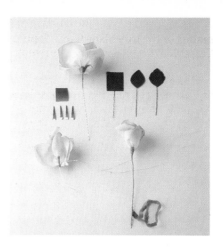

3 Make a bud by rolling two petals to form a centre and surrounding them with three petals wired in single-row sequence, as for the flower. Secure the bud to a stem wire and add sepals and leaves. Tape to the end of the stem.

The size and number of petals can be increased or decreased to make larger or smaller flowers. A stamen centre can be used in place of the petal centre.

MATERIALS
Shaded poplin ribbon in pink/cream

Acetate ribbon in green

Green stem tape

30-gauge wire

24-gauge green covered wire

18-gauge stem wire

36mm (1⁷⁄₁₆in) double-sided adhesive tape

1 Cut thirteen 72mm (2¹³⁄₁₆in) squares of shaded poplin ribbon and cut a petal shape from each one.

Stretch the petals at the centres between thumbs and forefingers to cup them slightly. Tool the top edges of the petals with the rose-petal curling head or roll the edges over a stem wire.

Roll two petals together to form a centre and secure by the twisting method using 30-gauge wire. Neaten with half-width green stem tape and join in an 18-gauge stem wire.

2 Cut five 5×40mm (³⁄₁₆×1⁹⁄₁₆in) rectangles from green acetate ribbon and cut sepals. Apply a very small piece of double-sided tape to the base of each sepal on the right side of the ribbon. Peel the backing paper from the double-sided tape and stick the sepals evenly around the top of the flower stem, just below the petal base. Tape to secure. Hold very firmly and curl the sepals downwards over closed scissor blades.

Cut ten 36×60mm (1⁷⁄₁₆×2³⁄₈in) rectangles of green acetate ribbon. On five pieces, apply double-sided tape to the matt side.

Cut five 100mm (3¹⁵⁄₁₆in) lengths of green covered wire. Attach a wire down the centre of each acetate rectangle. Cover with the other five rectangles.

Cut the leaf shapes and serrate the edges. Mark the leaf veins with scissor blades or the tool blade head.

Make a group of five leaves by taping them together with half-width green stem tape. Join the leaves to the flower stem with full-width tape and continue taping down the flower stem. (If the stem is long, it is advisable to add at least one other group of leaves.)

LENTEN ROSE
(Helleborus orientalis)

MATERIALS
Two-colour silky ribbon in wine red/mauve

Flocked ribbon in cream and yellow

Acetate ribbon in green

Cream pointed stamens

Stem tape in yellow and red-brown

30-gauge wire

26-gauge green covered wire

22-gauge stem wire

Double-sided adhesive tape in 5mm (³⁄₁₆in) and 36mm (⁷⁄₁₆in) widths

1 Cut ten 36mm (1⁷⁄₁₆in) squares of silky ribbon. Lay double-sided tape diagonally across the centre of each of five squares. Cut five 72mm (2¹³⁄₁₆in) lengths of green covered wire. Attach a wire to the centre of each strip of double-sided tape and cover with the remaining squares of silky ribbon. Cut the petal shapes and crinkle by the damp cloth method.

Finely fringe a 10×70mm (³⁄₈×2¾in) strip of cream flocked ribbon and a 15×60mm (⁹⁄₁₆×2³⁄₈in) strip of yellow flocked ribbon. Run 5mm (³⁄₁₆in) double-sided tape along the uncut edge of each fringe on the flocked side.

Make a hook at the end of a length of green covered wire and fasten it into the cream fringe. Remove the backing paper from the double-sided tape and roll the fringe onto the hook.

Apply double-sided tape to the base of the fringed centre. Cut fifteen stamens in half to make thirty short stamens. Remove the backing paper from the double-sided tape and press the stamens around the cream fringe. Remove the backing paper from the tape on the yellow fringe and roll this around the flower centre, flocked side inwards. Secure with yellow stem tape.

2 Curve the reinforcing wires on the petals and wire five petals in single-row sequence using 30-gauge

wire, making several twists of wire between each petal. Hold the petals around the flower centre and fasten with the long ends of 30-gauge wire. Join the long and short wires and twist the flower to secure. Cover with red-brown stem tape. Join in a 22-gauge stem wire and tape the stem with the red-brown tape.

Spread the stamens and fringes at the flower centre. Bend the stem just behind the flowerhead.

For a full spray, make five flowers in all, including one or two made with petals cut from 48mm (1⁷⁄₈in) squares.

3 Make a bud with three petals cut from 24mm (¹⁵⁄₁₆in) squares of shaded silky ribbon. Reinforce and line the petals as for the flower. Wire the petals in single-row sequence very tightly using 30-gauge wire.

There is no centre for the bud. Wrap the third petal around the first and take the long ends of 30-gauge wire twice around the bud base. Join in the short lengths and twist the bud to secure. Cut the wire ends short and cover with half-width red-brown tape. Curve the stem behind the bud head.

4 Cut two 65×72mm (2⁹⁄₁₆×2¹³⁄₁₆in) rectangles of green acetate ribbon. Lay 36mm

(1⁷⁄₁₆in) double-sided tape on the shiny side of one rectangle. Cut three 110mm (4⁵⁄₁₆in) lengths of green covered wire. Attach them to the double-sided tape, evenly spaced across the width of the rectangle. Cover with the second acetate ribbon rectangle, matt side up.

Cut three leaf shapes. Mark the leaf veins with scissor blades or the tool blade head. Join the leaves in a trefoil arrangement and tape them to the flower stem using red-brown stem tape.

Make two or more groups of leaves for each flower spray. Tape flowers, buds and leaves together to form a single-stemmed spray.

Cut three 24×36mm (¹⁵⁄₁₆×1⁷⁄₁₆in) rectangles of green acetate ribbon and shape sepals. Wrap one around the main stem at the point where a flower stem is joined in and secure by the twisting method using 30-gauge wire. Cut the wire short and neaten with stem tape. Attach the other sepals at stem joints in the same way.

MAGNOLIA

MATERIALS

Velvet silky ribbon in white and green
Silky ribbon in white
Flocked ribbon in yellow
Stem tape in red-brown and yellow
30-gauge wire
24-gauge white covered wire
20-gauge stem wire
Double-sided adhesive tape in 5mm (³⁄₁₆in) and 36mm (1⁷⁄₁₆in) widths
Pink chalk
Small natural tree branch

1 Cut six 36×72mm (1⁷⁄₁₆×2¹³⁄₁₆in) rectangles of white velvet ribbon and six of white silky ribbon. Apply 36mm (1⁷⁄₁₆in) double-sided tape to the wrong side of the velvet ribbon squares. Cut six 80mm (3⅛in) lengths of white covered wire. Attach a wire to the centre of each rectangle and cover with the rectangles of white silky.

Cut the petal shapes and stretch the ribbon around the petal tips. Colour the base of each petal heavily with pink chalk. Wire the base by the hairpin method using 30-gauge wire and neaten with red-brown stem tape.

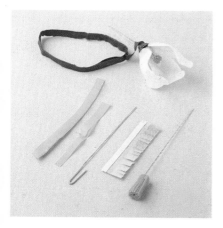

2 Cut a 20×72mm (¹³⁄₁₆×2¹³⁄₁₆in) rectangle of yellow flocked ribbon and apply 5mm (³⁄₁₆in) double-sided tape to one long edge of the ribbon on the wrong side. Fringe the opposite side finely. Cover one end of a 20-gauge stem wire with yellow stem tape and make a hook. Insert the hook in the fringe, remove the backing tape from the double-sided tape and roll the fringe evenly onto the hook. Trim the stem wire to a length of about 80mm (3⅛in).

Place three petals evenly spaced around the flower centre and fasten with full-width red-brown stem tape.

The base of each petal should sit below the yellow centre. Position the remaining three petals in the spaces between the first three and secure with tape.

3 Cut six 48×12mm (1⅞×⁷⁄₁₆in) rectangles of green velvet ribbon and shape sepals. Place three sepals around the flower, velvet side inwards and secure with red-brown stem tape. Hold the base of the sepals very firmly and stroke the tip of each one outwards over closed scissor blades.

Tape to the end of the stem. The flower may be left closed or opened out slightly by gently easing back the petals.

4 To make a bud, cut three 24×40mm (¹⁵⁄₁₆×1⁹⁄₁₆in) rectangles of white velvet ribbon and three of white silky ribbon. Reinforce and line these smaller rectangles as for the large flower and cut them as small petals. Stretch the petal tips.

Wire the base of each petal by the hairpin method and neaten with half-width red-brown stem tape.

Thicken one end of a short length of 20-gauge stem wire with yellow stem tape. Arrange the three petals around the centre and secure with red-brown stem tape. If you wish, attach two or three brown silky sepals to the bud with adhesive tape.

For the branch, make at least two flowers and two buds and attach them to the natural tree branch with stem tape. For a large branch, vary the flower sizes by increasing the length of the petals to 80mm (3⅛in), 90mm (3⁹⁄₁₆in) or 100mm (3¹⁵⁄₁₆in).

An alternative to using natural wood is to curve and join ends of 16-gauge padded craft wire; or tape together several 18-gauge stem wires, cover with brown tape and bend them into shape.

MICHAELMAS DAISY (Aster novi-belgii)

MATERIALS

Velvet silky or flocked ribbon in wine red and yellow

Acetate ribbon in green

Green stem tape

30-gauge wire

24-gauge green covered wire

20-gauge stem wire

5mm (³⁄₁₆in) double-sided adhesive tape

1 Cut a 9×72mm (⁵⁄₁₆×2¹³⁄₁₆in) strip of yellow velvet ribbon. Halve a piece of double-sided tape lengthwise and place a narrow strip

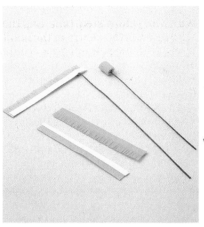

MINIATURE IRIS

of tape along one long edge of the ribbon. Fringe the opposite edge of the ribbon finely.

Make a hook at one end of a length of green covered wire. Hook it into the fringe, remove the backing paper from the double-sided tape and roll the fringe tightly on to the wire hook.

2 Cut a 24×72mm (^{15}⁄$_{16}$×2^{13}⁄$_{16}$in) rectangle of wine red velvet ribbon. Place a length of 5mm (^{3}⁄$_{16}$in) double-sided tape down one long edge and fringe the opposite edge finely.

Remove the backing paper from the double-sided tape and wrap the petal fringe velvet side inwards, around the flower centre, keeping the lower edges level. Secure by the twisting method using 30-gauge wire and neaten with stem tape. Curl the petals outwards from the centre over closed scissor blades.

Cut small leaflets from 3×30mm (^{1}⁄$_8$×1^3⁄$_{16}$in) pieces of green acetate ribbon. Tape them to the flower stem in pairs, shiny sides inwards. Finish by taping the stem.

To make a spray of Michaelmas daisies, assemble several florets in a loose grouping and attach them to a stem wire using green stem tape.

MATERIALS

Silky ribbon in purple and green
Green stem tape
30-gauge wire
30- and 24-gauge green covered wire
20-gauge stem wire
5mm (^{3}⁄$_{16}$in) double-sided adhesive tape
Flowermaking adhesive
Tissue paper

1 From purple silky ribbon, cut three 36×60mm (1^7⁄$_{16}$×2^3⁄$_8$in) rectangles, three 18×45mm (^{11}⁄$_{16}$×1^{13}⁄$_{16}$in) and three 15×36mm (^{9}⁄$_{16}$×1^7⁄$_{16}$in). Cut these into large, medium and small petals.

Crinkle all the petals by the damp cloth method and stretch them gently. Use flowermaking adhesive to attach a length of 30-gauge green covered wire to the centre of each petal.

2 Cover the end of a 20-gauge stem wire with green stem tape. Position the smallest three petals, wires on the outside, around the stem tip and secure with stem tape.

Position the three medium-sized petals, wires on the inside, in the spaces between the three small petals and tape them in place. Tape the three large petals in place, with the wires on the outside, so that they lie directly below the small petals.

Curve the petal wires gently so that the small and medium petals stand out from the stem and curve inwards and the large petals curve out and down from the flower base.

3 Tape the full stem. Thicken the flower stem by wrapping tissue paper around it down the full length and cover with stem tape.

Cut two 18×40mm (1^1⁄$_{16}$×1^9⁄$_{16}$in) rectangles of green silky ribbon and shape bracts. Crinkle by the damp cloth method. Place one bract on the stem with the tip just below the flower base. Secure with 30-gauge wire by the twisting method and neaten with stem tape. Position the second bract 20mm (^{13}⁄$_{16}$in) lower, on the opposite side of the stem and secure as before.

Cut a 24×110mm (¹⁵⁄₁₆×4⁵⁄₁₆in) rectangle of green silky ribbon. Fold it in half lengthwise and place a strip of double-sided tape down the centre on one side. Attach a length of 24-gauge green covered wire to the adhesive tape. Fold over the other half of the rectangle to line the first. Cut the leaf shape as shown.

To make the larger iris, double the petal and bract sizes given. When making a grouping of miniature iris, add several leaves of varying sizes.

MORNING GLORY (Ipomoea)

MATERIALS

Shaded silky ribbon in blue/white
Silky ribbon in white and green
Stem tape in green and yellow
30-gauge wire
30-gauge white covered wire
28- and 24-gauge green covered wire
20-gauge stem wire
36mm (1⁷⁄₁₆in) double-sided adhesive tape
Flowermaking adhesive

1 Cut a 72mm (2¹³⁄₁₆in) square of white silky ribbon. Fold and cut as shown to make petal A. Use adhesive to attach a length of white covered wire to each finger of the petal.

Cut five 55×72mm (2³⁄₁₆×2¹³⁄₁₆in) rectangles of shaded ribbon and shape petals B with the blue edge of the ribbon at the top of the petal and white at the base.

2 Hold petal A with the wires facing you and apply adhesive to the right-hand edge of one finger of petal A. Attach one petal B, with the narrowest overlap possible to secure the join. Repeat so that one petal B is attached to the right-hand side of each finger of petal A. Stick the free edge of each petal B to the left-hand edge of each finger of petal A and close up the circle of petals by sticking the free edge of the last petal B to the adjacent finger of petal A. Trim off any overlaps around the outer edge of the circle.

Dampen your fingers and gently stretch the petals to make a fluted effect.

Tape the end of a 20-gauge stem wire with yellow stem tape. Slip the wire through the centre of the petal circle, with the yellow tip protruding about 10mm (³⁄₈in). Tape the petal wires and main stem together to secure.

To make a bud, fold and roll a 72×120mm (2¹³⁄₁₆×4³⁄₄in) rectangle of shaded silky ribbon, as shown. Fold top over bottom and right side over left and roll from the right, rotating around the folded corner. Secure by the twisting method using 30-gauge wire. Neaten with green stem tape and tape the bud to a stem wire.

3 Cut a 48mm (1⁷⁄₈in) square of green silky ribbon and form a calyx by folding and cutting the square in the same way as for petal A. Wrap the calyx around the flower stem just below the base of the flower and secure with green stem tape.

Make a calyx for the bud and, when attaching it to the stem, allow the calyx to overlap the bud. Finish taping the bud and flower stems.

Cut two 72mm (2¹³⁄₁₆in), two 60mm (2³⁄₈in) and two 48mm (1⁷⁄₈in) squares of green silky ribbon. Take one square of each size and cover with double-sided tape. Attach a length of 24-gauge green covered wire diagonally and two smaller pieces on either side. Cover with the second silky ribbon square of the same size.

Cut one leaf from each square and mark the leaf veins with scissor blades or the tool blade head. Tape the three leaves together, leaving long leaf stems.

To assemble, attach the bud and leaf stems to the main flower stem with green stem tape and continue taping down the flower stem.

NERINE

MATERIALS
Silky ribbon in pink and green
Pink round stamens
Green stem tape
30-gauge wire
30-gauge white covered wire
18-gauge stem wire
Flowermaking adhesive

1 To make one floret, cut six 12×65mm (⁷⁄₁₆×2⁹⁄₁₆in) rectangles of pink silky ribbon and shape petals. Use adhesive to stick a 120mm (4¾in) length of white covered wire down the centre of each petal. Allow the adhesive to dry.

2 Tool down each wire from top to bottom of the petals with the smooth curved head to curl the petals naturally.

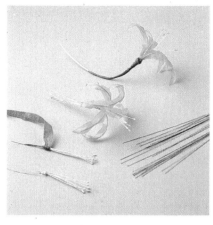

3 Assemble seven stamens and cut off the heads at one end. Secure the cut ends with half-width stem tape.

Position the petals around the stamen centre and secure by the twisting method using 30-gauge wire. Cover the wire with half-width stem tape. Continue taping to thicken the stem just below the floret and tape to the end of the floret stem.

4 For one flowerhead, make up six florets in all. Position them at the top of an 18-gauge stem wire and secure them in place with stem tape. Make sure that each floret stands 30mm (1³⁄₁₆in) from the main stem on its own stem. Tape down 20mm (¹³⁄₁₆in) of the main stem to hold the floret stems firmly and bend them gently outwards to make an evenly radiating pattern from the stem tip.

5 Cut two 12×50mm (⁷⁄₁₆×2in) rectangles of green silky ribbon and shape leaves. Attach the leaves to the main stem at the point where the florets are attached, on opposite sides of the stem. Secure by the twisting method, using 30-gauge wire. Neaten with stem tape and continue taping down the main stem.

ORCHID

MATERIALS
Shaded poplin ribbon in green/white
Stem tape in white and pale green
30-gauge wire
24-gauge white covered wire
18-gauge stem wire
Double-sided adhesive tape in 5mm (³⁄₁₆in) and 36mm (1⁷⁄₁₆in) widths
Dark red crayon or felt-tip pen

1 Cut six 36×72mm (1⁷⁄₁₆×2¹³⁄₁₆in) rectangles of shaded poplin ribbon. Cover three rectangles with 36mm (1⁷⁄₁₆in) double-sided tape and attach a 100mm (3¹⁵⁄₁₆in) length of white covered wire to the centre of each rectangle. Cover with the second ribbon rectangle. Cut one petal A from each.

Cut four 30×72mm (1³⁄₁₆×2¹³⁄₁₆in) rectangles from shaded poplin ribbon. Reinforce two rectangles with white covered wire as above and fully line each one with a second rectangle. Cut two petals B.

Tool the A and B petals from tip to base with the blade head. Gently stretch the outer edges between your fingers.

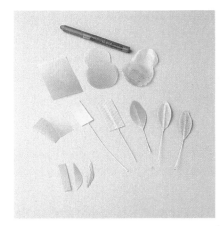

2 Cut a 44×70mm (1³⁄₄×2³⁄₄in) rectangle of shaded poplin ribbon and cut petal C. Tool the petal with the smooth curved head to turn in the top edges and turn back the lower edges. Stretch the bottom section between thumbs and forefingers. Colour the underside of the bottom section with the red crayon.

Cut two 8×36mm (⁹⁄₃₂×1⁷⁄₁₆in) rectangles and shape petals D.

Crinkle by the spiral twist method.

Cut two 20×43mm (¹³⁄₁₆×1¹¹⁄₁₆in) poplin ribbon rectangles. Reinforce one with white covered wire as above and line it fully with the second rectangle. Cut petal E. Mark about two-thirds of the petal surface with red dots. Tool the outer edges with the curved head to curl them slightly.

3 Cut a 30mm (1³⁄₁₆in) strip of 5mm (³⁄₁₆in) double-sided tape and cut it in half lengthwise. Apply a narrow strip to petal C, starting from the base. Use this to attach the petals D, very close together, to the base of petal C. Colour the centre with crayon or pen and pinch the petals to make them stand up from the centre join.

Place a short strip of 5mm (³⁄₁₆in) double-sided tape on the spotted side of petal E. Attach it to the base of petal C. Secure by the twisting method, using 30-gauge wire. Trim the wire ends short and neaten with half-width white stem tape.

Position one petal B on either side of the wired petals and secure with tape. Place one petal A at the top and two at the bottom of the petal group. Tape to secure and join in an 18-gauge stem wire using green stem tape.

Repeat to make a second flower.

Make a bud by taping together three petals B and attaching them to an 18-gauge stem wire. Join the flowers to the bud stem at intervals of about 70mm (2³⁄₄in) and continue taping the main stem.

PANSY (Viola)

MATERIALS

Velvet silky ribbon in yellow
Silky ribbon in yellow and green
Stem tape in yellow and green
30-gauge green covered wire
28-gauge white covered wire
20-gauge stem wire
5mm (³⁄₁₆in) double-sided adhesive tape
Flowermaking adhesive
Brown pencil or felt-tip pen

1 From velvet ribbon, cut a 36×60mm (1⁷⁄₁₆×2³⁄₈in) rectangle and shape petal A. Cut two 36×50mm (1⁷⁄₁₆×2in) rectangles and shape petals B. Cut two 36mm (1⁷⁄₁₆in) squares and shape petals C.

Lay a strip of double-sided tape down the back of each petal and attach a length of white covered wire. Strip line each petal with a narrow strip of yellow silky ribbon.

Mark the petal bases with the brown pencil or pen.

2 Thicken one end of a 20-gauge stem wire with yellow stem tape to form a node. Place petal A against the wire so that the node sits about 5mm (³⁄₁₆in) above the base of the petal. Secure with yellow stem tape.

Tape petals C to the stem about 5mm (³⁄₁₆in) below petal A. Bend the node slightly so that the petals form the pansy face.

Attach petals B just below petals C, arranged to overlap A and C at the back of the flower. Secure all the petals with half-width green stem tape.

3 Cut a 36mm (1⁷⁄₁₆in) square of green silky ribbon and cut the calyx. Use small pieces of double-sided tape to attach it to the stem, overlapping the flower base.

Cut five 24×50mm (¹⁵⁄₁₆×2in) rectangles of green silky ribbon and shape leaves. Use adhesive to attach a length of green covered wire to the back of each leaf. Mark the leaf veins with scissor blades or the tool blade head.

Tape the leaf bases with half-width green stem tape and join them to the flower stem. Bend the leaf stems slightly so that the leaves spread out and down the main stem.

PELARGONIUM

MATERIALS

Silky ribbon in pale pink and green
Green stem tape
33-gauge white covered wire
28-gauge green covered wire
20-gauge stem wire
Double-sided adhesive tape in 5mm (³⁄₁₆in) and 36mm (1⁷⁄₁₆in) widths
Purple crayon
Brown felt-tip pen

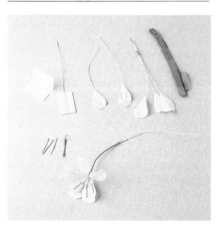

1 Cut five 30×36 mm (1³⁄₁₆×1⁷⁄₁₆in) rectangles of pink silky ribbon. Fold in half and place a strip of 5mm (³⁄₁₆in) double-sided tape down the centre of one half of each rectangle. Attach a length of white covered wire to each strip and fold over the other half of the rectangle to line the first. Cut five petals.

Mark two petals near the base with two purple lines. Stretch the tips of all five petals.

Use purple crayon to colour a length of white covered wire and cut three 20mm (¹³⁄₁₆in) lengths to use as stamens. Tape the stamens together with half-width green stem tape.

Assemble the petals around the stamen centre, with the two purple-striped petals side by side and secure with half-width stem tape.

Repeat to make a second flower.

2 Cut a 72×110mm (2¹³⁄₁₆×4⁵⁄₁₆in) rectangle of green silky ribbon. Fold it in half lengthways and cover one half with 36mm (1⁷⁄₁₆in) double-sided tape.

Cut five lengths of green covered wire and attach them to the double-sided tape in a radial pattern, coming together about 10mm (³⁄₈in) from the edge of the rectangle. Fold over the second half of the rectangle, slitting the edge of the ribbon to ease it round the wires. Cut the leaf shape.

Mark the leaf veins with scissor blades or the tool blade head and colour the edge of the leaf with brown felt-tip pen.

Make leaves in pairs and join the pairs together with green stem tape to form a single stem about 50mm (2in) below the leaf bases.

Cut a 10×24mm (³⁄₈×¹⁵⁄₁₆in) rectangle of green silky ribbon, fold it in three and shape the calyx. Cut three calyces for each flower and two for each pair of leaves. Attach them to the edge of the strip of 5mm (³⁄₁₆in) double-sided tape in groups, leaving space for cutting. Lay a second strip of double-sided tape on top.

Attach the calyces to the stems where leaves or flowers join. Arrange the flowers and leaves into a spray and secure with green stem tape. Join in a 20-gauge stem wire if necessary to strengthen the main stem. Finish off the taping.

Make smaller leaves from 45×60mm (1¹³⁄₁₆×2³⁄₈in) and 30×45mm (1³⁄₁₆×1¹³⁄₁₆in) rectangles.

PEONY
(Paeonia)

MATERIALS

Shaded poplin ribbon in pink/white
Silky ribbon in cream
Acetate ribbon in green
Stem tape in white, light green and dark green
30-gauge wire
26-gauge white covered wire
26-gauge green covered wire
18-gauge stem wire
Double-sided adhesive tape in 5mm (3/16in) and 36mm (17/16in) widths
Flowermaking adhesive

1 Cut ten 72×80mm (2¹³/₁₆×3⅛in) rectangles of shaded poplin ribbon and shape petals. Cup and stretch them by pulling with both hands. Cut ten 100mm (3¹⁵/₁₆in)

lengths of white covered wire and use adhesive to stick one to the centre of each petal, starting about 30mm (1³/₁₆in) from the top. Leave the adhesive to dry.

Wire the petals together in double-row sequence, using 30-gauge wire.

2 Cut six 36×72mm (1⁷/₁₆×2¹³/₁₆in) rectangles of cream silky ribbon. Fold each one in four widthways and cut the petaloid shape as shown. Tool from tip to base of each section using the smooth curved head.

Hairpin wire the base of each petaloid with 30-gauge wire, leaving a short stem of about 40mm (1⁹/₁₆in). Neaten with half-width light green stem tape.

Cut three 100mm (3¹⁵/₁₆in) lengths of green covered wire. Tape the top of each one with white stem tape to thicken about 5mm (³/₁₆in). Tape another 15mm (⁹/₁₆in) of wire with half-width light green tape. From this point, join the three lengths together and secure with tape to form the flower centre.

3 Position the wired petaloids around the flower centre at the point where three stems are joined. Secure with half-width stem tape

and join in an 18-gauge stem wire. Tape down the stem.

Wrap the wired petals around the petaloids, taking the long ends of 30-gauge wire right around the petal bases. Hold together the long and short ends of wire and twist the flowerhead to secure. Trim the 30-gauge wires and neaten with half-width light green stem tape.

4 Cut two 72mm (2¹³/₁₆in) squares of green acetate ribbon. Apply 36mm (1⁷/₁₆in) double-sided tape to the matt side of one square. Attach three 80mm (3⅛in) lengths of green covered wire, evenly spaced across the square, and line with the second acetate square.

Cut three bracts, each with a wire down the centre. Mark the veins with scissor blades or the tool blade head.

Position the three bracts about 15mm (⁹/₁₆in) below the flower and secure to the main stem with full-width dark green stem tape. Continue taping down the flower stem.

To make leaves, work in the same way as for the bracts, using 72×80mm (2¹³/₁₆×3⅛in) rectangles of green acetate ribbon. Tape the leaf stems with half-width dark green stem tape and make a separate leaf stem by taping one leaf to the end of an 18-gauge stem wire. Attach the other leaves in pairs down the stem. The leaf stem can be joined to the main flower stem.

PETUNIA

MATERIALS

Silky ribbon in deep pink and green
Yellow stamens
Stem tape in green and yellow
33-gauge white covered wire
30-gauge wire
24-gauge green covered wire
20-gauge stem wire
5mm (³⁄₁₆in) double-sided adhesive tape
Flowermaking adhesive
Yellow crayon

1 Cut five 55×85mm (2³⁄₁₆×3³⁄₈in) rectangles of deep pink silky ribbon and shape petals. Crinkle by the spiral twist method.

Place a strip of double-sided tape down the centre of each petal and attach a length of white covered wire. Strip line each wire with a narrow strip of pink silky ribbon tapered at one end to a narrower width than that of the petal base.

Apply adhesive to one edge of each petal and join the petals together to form a circle, using the narrowest possible seam allowance. Keep the reinforcing wires on the outside of the circle.

2 Colour the centre of the flower with yellow crayon. (If this is done before the petals are stuck together, the ribbon becomes discoloured.)

Fold three stamen strings and cut in half. Take five heads and secure them with yellow stem tape. Attach the stamen centre to a 20-gauge stem wire with yellow tape.

Slip the stem wire into the throat of the flower. Secure the flower base by the twisting method using 30-gauge wire. Neaten with half-width green stem tape.

To make a bud, stick five wired petals together with the wires on the inside, insert the stamen centre as for the flower and close up the petals. Secure by the twisting method and tape at least 25mm (1in) of the bud base.

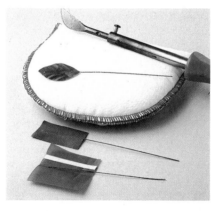

3 Cut a 52×56mm (2¹⁄₁₆×2¼in) rectangle of green silky ribbon, fold it in half and apply double-sided tape to the centre of one half. Attach a length of 24-gauge green covered wire and fold over the second half of the rectangle to line the first. Cut the leaf shape. Mark the leaf veins with the tool blade head or with scissor blades.

For one flower stem, make several leaves gradually increasing in size.

To assemble, tape down the flower stem and join in the bud stem. Attach the leaves at intervals in pairs, increasing in size down the stem.

POINSETTIA (Euphorbia pulcherrima)

MATERIALS

Velvet silky ribbon in bright red and green
Silky ribbon in bright red and green
Red berry stamens
Stem tape in yellow, light green and green
24-gauge green covered wire
Double-sided adhesive tape in 24mm (¹⁵⁄₁₆in) and 36mm (1⁷⁄₁₆in) widths

1 Cut five 24×72mm (¹⁵⁄₁₆×2¹³⁄₁₆in) and five 36×90mm (1⁷⁄₁₆×3⁹⁄₁₆in) rectangles of red velvet ribbon. Cut five 36×90mm (1⁷⁄₁₆×3⁹⁄₁₆in) rectangles of green velvet ribbon.

Cut the same number of rectangles of the same sizes in red and green silky ribbon.

Cover the wrong side of each velvet ribbon rectangle with double-sided tape. Attach a length of green covered wire to the centre of each rectangle and fully line with the appropriate piece of silky ribbon.

Cut a bract shape from each rectangle and crinkle all bracts using the spiral twist method.

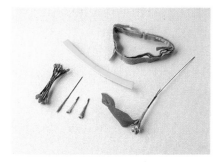

2 Cut five red berry stamens in half. Tape with half-width yellow stem tape covering just over half of each stamen head. Tape again with half-width light green stem tape, allowing a narrow strip of yellow to show at the top edge.

Cut twelve 60mm (2⅜in) lengths of green covered wire and tape each at one end with half-width light green stem tape to form a node.

Assemble the berry stamens and green nodes into five groups and tape one group to each small red bract using half-width light green stem tape. Allow 10mm (⅜in) of the stamen stems to stand free. Tape the small bracts together using full-width green stem tape.

3 Attach the large red bracts below the small ones, filling the spaces between. Tape the green bracts below the large red bracts as above. Tape the wires together to form a single stem.

To make the small poinsettia, cut bracts from 24×36mm (15⁄16×1⅞16in) and 24×48mm (15⁄16×1⅞in) rectangles. For the metallic ribbon version, cut all bracts from 24×72mm (15⁄16×2¹³⁄16in) rectangles; this should be lined with silky ribbon.

POMPON DAHLIA

MATERIALS
Acetate ribbon in red and green
Velvet silky or flocked ribbon in yellow
Green stem tape
33- and 28-gauge green covered wire
30-gauge wire
18-gauge stem wire
Double-sided adhesive tape in 5mm (³⁄16in) and 24mm (15⁄16in) widths

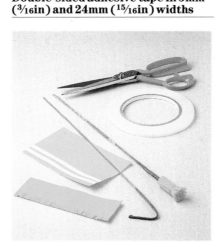

1 Cut a 72×120mm (2¹³⁄16×4¾in) rectangle of yellow velvet ribbon. Fold it in half lengthwise and crease the fold. Open out the ribbon and place two strips of 5mm (³⁄16in) double-sided tape along one long edge. Fold back the other side and secure to the adhesive tape. Fringe to a depth of about 10mm (⅜in) from the folded edge.

Tape two 18-gauge stem wires together and form a hook at one end. Hook it into one end of the fringe and squeeze with pliers to secure. Roll up the fringe very tightly and secure the base by the twisting method, using 30-gauge wire. Neaten with green stem tape.

2 From red acetate ribbon cut eight 24×30mm (15⁄16×1³⁄16in), twelve 24×36mm (15⁄16×1⁷⁄16in), fourteen 30×44mm (1³⁄16×1¾in) and sixteen 36×48mm (1⁷⁄16×1⅞in) rectangles. Cut the petal shapes to make four groups of petals.

Wire each group of petals in single-row sequence using 30-gauge wire. Fold each petal in exactly the same way, without creasing, and only as it is needed. Hold each petal firmly at the base but allow the top to stand naturally.

3 Wrap the sequence of small petals around the flower centre. Wrap the long ends of 30-gauge wire around the petal bases, hold the long and short wires together and twist the flowerhead to secure. Neaten with green stem tape.

Add the sequence of medium-sized petals in the same way, followed by the two sets of large petals.

4 Cut ten 24×36mm ($^{15}/_{16}$×1$^{7}/_{16}$in) rectangles of green acetate ribbon and shape sepals. Fold them in half widthways and wire them together in single-row sequence using 33-gauge green covered wire, slipping one wire into each fold.

Wrap the wired sepals around the flower base, twist the flower to secure the wires and cut them short. Neaten with green stem tape and tape down the flower stem.

5 Cut three 72×96mm (2$^{13}/_{16}$×3$^{13}/_{16}$in) rectangles of green acetate ribbon. Fold each one in half widthways and cover one side with double-sided tape. Attach a length of 24-gauge green covered wire across the diagonal of the taped half and fold down the other half of the ribbon to line the first. Cut the leaf shapes.

Mark the leaf veins with the tool blade head or with scissor blades. Tape two leaves together and join in the single and paired leaves to the flower stem.

To make a smaller flower, omit the fourth row of petals. On a long stem, vary the leaf sizes to create a natural effect.

POPPY (Papaver)

MATERIALS
Silky ribbon in bright red and green
Black stamens
Stem tape in black and green
30-gauge wire
30 and 24-gauge green covered wire
18-gauge stem wire
36mm (1$^{7}/_{16}$in) double-sided adhesive tape

1 Cut eight 72mm (2$^{13}/_{16}$in) squares of bright-red silky ribbon and shape petals. Crinkle by the damp cloth method. Stretch the edges gently between your fingers and cup the petal centres.

Hairpin wire the base of each petal and neaten with half-width green stem tape.

2 Assemble twelve lengths of 30-gauge green covered wire and tape them together at the centre

with black stem tape. Thicken with tape to form a pod. Turn the wires evenly back over the pod from one end and secure below the pod with green stem tape.

Make up four groups of sixteen stamen strings, fold them in half and secure with 30-gauge wire. Cluster the stamens around the pod and secure by the twisting method using 30-gauge wire. Neaten with green stem tape.

Join in two lengths of 18-gauge stem wire to form a stem below the flower centre. Secure with green stem tape.

Place two petals on opposite sides of the flower centre and secure with stem tape. Position the next two petals to cover the spaces between the first two and tape. Repeat with the remaining four petals to form the full flower.

Tape down the flower stem to the point where leaves will be joined.

3 Cut two 72×125mm (2$^{13}/_{16}$×4$^{15}/_{16}$in) rectangles of green silky ribbon. Cover one with double-sided tape and attach a length of 24-gauge covered wire. Cover with the second rectangle and cut the leaf shape as shown.

Mark the leaf veins with the tool blade head or with scissor blades. Tape the base of the leaf with half-width green stem tape.

Make at least three leaves per flower stem and tape them to the stem at intervals on alternate sides.

Ready-made leaves can be used for the poppy, reinforced and taped at the base before joining to the stem.

PRIMULA

MATERIALS

Velvet silky ribbon in pale pink
Acetate ribbon in green
Yellow stamens
Green stem tape
24-gauge green covered wire
5mm (³⁄₁₆in) double-sided adhesive tape
Flowermaking adhesive
Yellow felt-tip pen

1 Cut four 36mm (1⁷⁄₁₆in) squares of velvet ribbon. Fold each square by the five-point fold and cut

as shown. Unfold the squares and cut the petal indentations slightly deeper towards the centre of the flower.

2 Hold a flower in one hand and twist each petal section in a clockwise direction with the other hand. Open out the flower. Tool the centre with the small ball head. Make a small hole in the centre with a darning needle, without pulling the needle right through the ribbon.

Colour the centre of the flower with yellow felt-tip pen. Repeat with each flower.

3 Cut a stamen string in half and put a small dab of adhesive on one stamen just below the head. Push the stamen stem through the hole in the flower and position the head at the centre of the flower.

Tape the stem of the flowerhead to a short length of green covered wire. Continue taping down about half of the wire stem.

Make the other flowers.

4 Cut a 36×65mm (1⁷⁄₁₆×2⁹⁄₁₆in) rectangle of green acetate ribbon and shape the leaf. Fold it in half and crinkle by the damp cloth method. Cut a narrow strip of green acetate ribbon and cover with

double-sided tape. Attach a length of green covered wire to the tape and strip-line the centre of the matt side of the leaf.

Make at least three pairs of leaves for one flower cluster and vary the sizes between each pair. Smaller and larger leaves can be made from 30×60mm (1³⁄₁₆×2³⁄₈in) and 48×80mm (1⁷⁄₈×3¹⁄₈in) rectangles.

Assemble the flowers and leaves in a cluster and tape the stem ends together.

SCABIOUS

MATERIALS

Silky ribbon in pale mauve and green
Bright green stem tape
33-gauge green covered wire
30-gauge wire
20-gauge stem wire
Flowermaking adhesive

1 Cut fifteen 18×24mm (¹¹⁄₁₆×¹⁵⁄₁₆in) rectangles of mauve silky ribbon and shape petals A. Cut eighteen 18×36mm (¹¹⁄₁₆×1⁷⁄₁₆in) rectangles of mauve silky ribbon and shape petals B. Crinkle by the spiral twist method.

47

Wire petals A together in a single-row sequence, using 30-gauge wire. Repeat with petals B.

2 Cut one hundred and eighty 36mm (1⁷⁄₁₆in) lengths of green covered wire. Thicken 5mm (³⁄₁₆in) at one end of each wire with quarter-width green stem tape to form stamen heads. Tape all the stamens together at the base and join in a 20-gauge wire on either side of the stamen centre.

Wrap the wired petals A around the stamen centre. Pull the 30-gauge wires tightly and twist the flower to secure. Neaten with stem tape.

Add the wired petals B in the same way. Neaten with stem tape and continue taping down the stem.

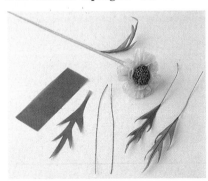

3 Cut two 36×110mm (1⁷⁄₁₆×4⁵⁄₁₆in) rectangles of green silky ribbon and shape leaves. Use adhesive to stick a length of green covered wire down the centre of each leaf. Mark the leaf veins with scissor blades or the tool blade head.

Tape the base of each leaf with half-width green stem tape and tape them to opposite sides of the flower stem.

SCILLA

MATERIALS

Acetate ribbon in blue and green
Blue round stamens
Stem tape in blue and green
30-gauge wire
20-gauge stem wire
24mm (¹⁵⁄₁₆in) double-sided adhesive tape

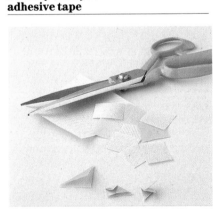

1 Cut nine 24mm (¹⁵⁄₁₆in) squares of blue acetate ribbon. Fold each square as shown and cut the petal shape through all the layers to make a floret.

2 Open out the folds and tool the centre of each floret, shiny side up, with the small ball head. Pierce the centre with a darning needle or fine wire. Tool the individual petal sections from tip to centre with the smooth curved head.

Fold a stamen string in half and push the folded end through the centre of the floret to leave the stamen heads pressed against the ribbon centre. Tape the stamen stem with half-width blue stem tape. Apply stamens to all the florets in the same way.

Group the florets by taping all the stems at the base with half-width green stem tape. Join in a length of 20-gauge stem wire and tape. Spread the florets to make a rounded flowerhead.

3 Cut two 24×130mm (¹⁵⁄₁₆×5⅛in) rectangles of green acetate ribbon. Apply double-sided tape to the shiny side of one rectangle. Line it with the second rectangle, matt side upwards.

Cut the leaf shape and mark parallel veins vertically with scissor blades or the ridged tool head.

Attach a leaf to the base of the flower stem by the twisting method, using 30-gauge wire. Neaten with green stem tape.

You can attach leaves of varying sizes to the flower stem. If making a group of flowerheads, vary also the number of florets on each stem.

SMALL ROSE

MATERIALS

Silky ribbon in yellow
Acetate ribbon in green
Green stem tape
30-gauge wire
24-gauge green covered wire
18-gauge stem wire
24mm (¹⁵⁄₁₆in) double-sided adhesive tape
Flowermaking adhesive
Cotton wool

1 Cut twelve 48mm (1⅞in) squares of yellow silky ribbon and shape petals. Curl back the top edges by tooling with the rose petal curling head or roll the edges over a wire. Turn over the petals and cup the centres between thumbs and forefingers or tool with the small mushroom head.

Form a piece of cotton wool into a bud shape. Use flowermaking adhesive to stick one petal around the cotton wool bud to enclose it. Allow the adhesive to dry.

Stick one petal on either side of the cotton wool centre, applying adhesive over half of each petal, followed by three petals evenly spaced.

Stick another three petals to the flower base, using less adhesive so the petals open out a little from the previous layer. Repeat with the remaining three petals and allow the adhesive to dry.

Secure the base of the flower with 30-gauge wire by the twisting method. Neaten with half-width green stem tape and join in a length of 18-gauge stem wire.

2 Cut five 5×40mm (³⁄₁₆×1⁹⁄₁₆in) rectangles of green acetate and cut sepals. Attach small pieces of double-sided tape to the bases and press the sepals around the flower base, shiny side inwards. Secure with green stem tape and curve the sepals gently downwards with closed scissor blades.

Cut ten 24×45mm (¹⁵⁄₁₆×1¹³⁄₁₆in) rectangles of green acetate ribbon. On five rectangles, apply double-sided tape to the matt side. Attach an 80mm (3⅛in) length of green covered wire to the centre of each taped rectangle and cover with a second rectangle of acetate. Cut the leaf shapes.

Serrate the leaf edges and mark the leaf veins with scissor blades or the tool blade head.

Group the leaves as shown, with one at the tip of the leaf stem and two pairs below. Secure the stems with green stem tape and join the leaves to the flower stem.

To make a bud, proceed as for making the rose, but using only six petals. The size of the rose can be varied by increasing or decreasing the size and number of petals.

SNOWDROP (Galanthus nivalis)

MATERIALS

Velvet silky ribbon in white
Acetate ribbon in white
Silky ribbon in green
White round stamens
Green stem tape
30-gauge wire
26-gauge green covered wire
5mm (³⁄₁₆in) double-sided adhesive tape
Green felt-tip pen

1 Cut three 12×30mm (⁷⁄₁₆×1³⁄₁₆in) rectangles of white velvet ribbon and shape petals A.

Cut three 12×20mm (⁷⁄₁₆×1³⁄₁₆in) rectangles of white acetate ribbon and shape petals B. Colour the tips on the shiny side of the ribbon with a green felt-tip pen.

Wire together petals A and B alternately in double-row sequence, using 30-gauge wire, starting with a petal B. Keep the wrong side of the ribbon facing you with both types of petal.

2 Fold a stamen string in half and tape the folded end to a length of 26-gauge green covered wire, with the stamen heads standing about 10mm (³⁄₈in) above the wire.

Wrap the wired petals around the stamen centre, with the acetate petals on the inside and the velvet petals outside. Pulling tightly, wrap one length of wire round the flowerhead and cover 30mm (1³⁄₁₆in) of wires with half-width green stem tape.

Cut a 12×30mm (⁷⁄₁₆×1³⁄₁₆in) rectangle of green silky ribbon and cut the bract. Tape the bract to the stem below the flower base.

Cut two 10×72mm (³⁄₈×2¹³⁄₁₆in) rectangles of green silky ribbon. Place double-sided tape down one half of each rectangle and fold over the other half to line the first. Cut one leaf from each lined rectangle.

Tape the leaves to the base of the flower stem and finish off the stem with tape.

SPIDER CHRYSANTHEMUM

MATERIALS

Lantern ribbon in golden yellow

Pre-cut velvet chrysanthemum leaves

Green stem tape

30-gauge wire

20-gauge stem wire

5mm (³⁄₁₆in) double-sided adhesive tape

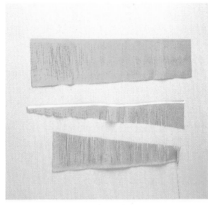

1 From a 500mm (19³⁄₄in) length of lantern ribbon cut diagonally down the length. (One flower can be made from each half of the ribbon.) Attach double-sided tape to the long straight edge of one piece.

2 Tape one end of a 20-gauge stem wire and bend it to form a hook. Hook it into the ribbon fringe at the narrow end. Remove the backing paper from the adhesive tape and squeeze the hook to secure the ribbon end. Roll the fringe very tightly and evenly around the wire hook. Secure the roll at the base of the fringe with 30-gauge wire by the twisting method.

Neaten with full-width green stem tape and join in a second length of 20-gauge stem wire. Secure with tape.

Curl the fringed petals over closed scissor blades.

Cover the leaf stems with half-width green stem tape. Tape down the flower stem and join in the leaves at intervals. Finish taping the stem.

SPIKY DAHLIA

MATERIALS

Acetate ribbon in pink and green

Green stem tape

33- and 24-gauge green covered wire

30-gauge wire

18-gauge stem wire

36mm (1⁷⁄₁₆in) double-sided adhesive tape

1 From pink acetate ribbon, cut twelve 24×50mm (¹⁵⁄₁₆×2in) rectangles, fifteen 24×60mm (¹⁵⁄₁₆×2³⁄₈in) and eighteen 24×70mm (¹⁵⁄₁₆×2³⁄₄in). Cut the petal shape from each rectangle to make groups of small, medium and large petals.

Fold in the bottom corners of one small petal to make a tube at the base, with the shiny side of the ribbon inwards. Wire the small petals, in single-row sequence, folding each one in exactly the same way. Hold the petal firmly at the base and allow the top to stand naturally. Leave a generous allowance of ribbon below the wire and make sure it is regular in each petal.

Repeat with the group of medium-sized petals and the group of large petals, so you have three wired rows.

2 Tape together two lengths of 18-gauge stem wire. Cover about half the length with tape and form a long hook at one end. Insert the hook between the second and third petals of the wired row of small petals and use pliers to close it firmly. Roll the petals around the hook tightly, with the folds facing inwards. Secure by wrapping the long ends of 30-gauge wire round the centre. Hold the short and long wires together firmly and twist the flowerhead. Neaten with green stem tape.

Wrap the row of medium-sized petals tightly around the small petals and secure in the same way. Repeat with the row of large petals. Neaten the flower base with stem tape.

3 Cut ten 24×36mm ($^{15}/_{16}$×1$^7/_{16}$in) rectangles of green acetate ribbon and shape sepals. Fold them in half widthways and wire in single-row sequence using 33-gauge green covered wire, sliding the wire into the fold each time. Wrap the sepals around the petals. Secure by holding wires firmly and twisting the flower. Trim the wires and neaten with stem tape.

4 Cut two 72×96mm (2$^{13}/_{16}$×3$^{13}/_{16}$in) rectangles of green acetate ribbon. Fold in half widthways, shiny side outwards, and attach double-sided tape to one half inside the fold. Lay a length of 24-gauge green covered wire diagonally across the taped half. Fold down the other half of the rectangle to line the first. Cut a leaf shape from each rectangle on the diagonal. Mark the leaf veins with scissor blades or the tool blade head.

Tape the leaves to the flower stem and tape to finish off the stem.

A smaller flower can be made using small and medium-sized petals only. If you are adding several leaves to a stem, vary the sizes to give a natural effect.

SPRING BLOSSOM

MATERIALS

Silky ribbon in pink, white and green
Yellow round stamens
Stem tape in green and dark brown
30-gauge wire
18-gauge stem wire
5mm (³/₁₆in) double-sided adhesive tape
Cotton wool

1 Cut one 36mm (1$^7/_{16}$in) square from each of the pink and white silky ribbons. Fold by the five-point fold method and cut the floret. Fold each floret in four and crinkle by the spiral twist method.

Open out the florets and place a small piece of double-sided tape near the centre of the pink floret. Attach the white floret to the tape, slightly off-centre. Make a hole at the centre through both layers, using a darning needle or fine wire.

2 Fold twelve stamen strings in half and secure the base with 30-gauge wire. Neaten the wire with green stem tape to form a short stem.

Push the stamen centre through the hole in the double floret, with the white floret uppermost, so that the stamen heads project about 10mm (³/₈in) from the floret centre. Secure the base of the floret by the twisting method using 30-gauge wire. Leave a wire stem about 30mm (1³/₁₆in) long and neaten with half-width green stem tape.

Make at least ten florets for one blossom twig. Two or three can be made all-white or all-pink.

To make a bud, cover a small ball of cotton wool with pink silky ribbon. Fasten the base with 30-

gauge wire by the twisting method and neaten with half-width green stem tape.

Alternatively, cut one floret from a 24mm (¹⁵⁄₁₆in) square of silky and crinkle as above. Fold it into a triangle and secure as for the cotton wool bud.

3 Cut a 36mm (1⁷⁄₁₆in) square of green silky ribbon, fold it diagonally and cut the calyx as shown. Join two florets with stem tape and wrap the calyx around the stem join. Secure by the twisting method, using 30-gauge wire. Trim the wire ends and neaten with green stem tape.

To make a short spray of blossom, join and tape 18-gauge stem wires to the required thickness with brown stem tape and attach the blossom stems. Alternatively secure the blossoms to a natural dry twig using twig stem tape.

STEPHANOTIS

MATERIALS
Silky ribbon in white and green
Green stem tape
30-gauge wire
5mm (³⁄₁₆in) double-sided adhesive tape

1 Cut five 10×20mm (³⁄₈×¹³⁄₁₆in) rectangles of white silky ribbon and cut petals.

Cut a 20×40mm (¹³⁄₁₆×1⁹⁄₁₆in) rectangle of white silky ribbon. Lay double-sided tape along two adjacent sides.

Attach the petals to the adhesive tape on the 20mm (¹³⁄₁₆in) side of the rectangle. Start from the left-hand side and stop 3mm (¹⁄₈in) short of the right-hand corner.

Roll the rectangle into a tube and secure with the double-sided tape on the long edge. It may be helpful to use a knitting needle to roll the tube evenly.

2 Open out the petals and stand the floret petals downwards on the work surface. Tool the petals with the smooth curved head.

Secure the bottom of the tube by the twisting method, using 30-gauge wire. Leave a stem of wire and tape with half-width green stem tape.

Cut a 24mm (¹⁵⁄₁₆in) square of green silky ribbon. Fold by the five-point fold and cut as shown to make the calyx.

Make a hole in the centre of the calyx and push it onto the flower stem under the base of the floret. Secure with half-width green stem tape.

Make three or more florets and tape them together to form a single-stemmed spray.

STOCK (Matthiola)

MATERIALS
Silky ribbon in pink and green
Cream stamens
Green stem tape
30-gauge wire
24-gauge green covered wire
20-gauge stem wire
Cotton wool

1 From pink silky ribbon, cut squares of 72mm (2¹³⁄₁₆in), 48mm (1⁷⁄₈in) and 36mm (1⁷⁄₁₆in). Fold each square by the five-point fold and cut as shown to make a large, medium and small petal. Tool at the centre and top edge of each section of the petal with the small ball head.

2 Fold three stamen strings and secure with 30-gauge wire. Neaten with half-width stem tape.

Make a hole in the centre of the small petal. Insert the stem of the stamen centre and push the petal right up to the base of the stamens. Secure by the twisting method, using 30-gauge wire and neaten with stem tape.

Attach the medium and large petals in the same way, making sure no stem tape is visible between the petals. Cover the stem wires with tape.

The three petals form a large flower. To make a small flower, use only the small and medium-sized petals: to make a medium-sized flower, use only the medium and large petals.

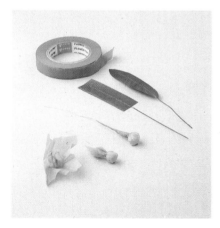

3 To make a bud, form a small ball of cotton wool and cover it with a square of pink silky ribbon. Secure by the twisting method, using 30-gauge wire and neaten with stem tape.

To make a closed bud, thicken the end of a 20-gauge stem wire with green stem tape.

Cut a 24×72mm ($^{15}/_{16}$×$2^{13}/_{16}$in) rectangle of green silky ribbon. Fold in half and lay double-sided tape on one half. Attach a length of green

covered wire to the centre of the taped half. Fold over the other half of the rectangle to line the first. Cut the leaf shape. Crinkle by the spiral twist method.

To make the flowerhead as shown, make two of each type of bud, two small and two medium florets and four large florets. Tape them to a stem of 20-gauge wire and attach leaves below the flowerhead. Leaves may vary in size up to 200mm ($7^{7}/_{8}$in).

SWEET PEA (Lathyrus)

MATERIALS

Silky ribbon in pink and green
Green stem tape
30-gauge wire
28-gauge green covered wire
20-gauge stem wire
5mm ($^{3}/_{16}$in) double-sided adhesive tape
Flowermaking adhesive
Cotton wool

1 Cut a 24mm ($^{15}/_{16}$in) square of pink silky ribbon and shape petal A. Fold it in half, fill the centre with

cotton wool and secure the edges with adhesive.

Cut two 36×48mm ($1^{7}/_{16}$×$1^{7}/_{8}$in) rectangles of pink silky ribbon. Cut petal B from one rectangle.

2 Stretch the edges of petal B. Apply adhesive to the folded edge of petal A and attach it to the centre of petal B, with the point at the top.

Cut one petal C from the second rectangle of silky ribbon and stretch the edges. Make a pleat down the centre and secure with adhesive.

Attach petal C to petals A and B by wrapping 30-gauge wire around the base: It is not necessary to twist the wires. Neaten with quarter-width stem tape.

3 Cut a 24mm ($^{15}/_{16}$in) square of green silky ribbon. Fold by the five-point fold and cut as shown to make a calyx. Tool with the smooth curved foot, working from tips to centre.

Make a small hole at the centre of the calyx with a darning needle or fine wire. Push the calyx up the flower stem to the base of the flower and secure with quarter-width stem tape.

Make a bud by cutting and filling one petal A, as above. Wire the base with 30-gauge wire and neaten with stem tape. Attach a calyx to the bud.

To make a small flower, use only petals A and B.

Cut a 30×36mm (1³⁄₁₆×1⁷⁄₁₆in) rectangle of green silky ribbon. Fold in half and apply double-sided tape down the centre of one half. Attach a length of green covered wire to the double-sided tape and fold over the other half of the silky to line the first. Cut the leaf shape. Make two leaves.

To make the tendril, cover a length of 30-gauge wire with quarter-width green stem tape and wrap this around a 20-gauge stem wire. Slide off the 30-gauge wire to form a loose, coiled spring effect. Cut to length required. Tape together the tendril and the pair of leaves.

To form a spray, tape one bud, one small flower and two large flowers to a 20-gauge stem wire. Cover the stem with green stem tape and tape in two leaves and a tendril below the flower.

TIGER LILY AND WHITE LILY

MATERIALS

Shaded silky ribbon in white/yellow
Poplin ribbon in white
Silky ribbon in green
Stem tape in brown, white, yellow and green
33- and 28-gauge white covered wire
30-gauge wire
28-gauge green covered wire
26-gauge yellow covered wire
20-gauge stem wire
5mm (³⁄₁₆in) double-sided adhesive tape
Flowermaking adhesive
Brown felt-tip pen

1 Cut six 36×72mm (1⁷⁄₁₆×2¹³⁄₁₆in) rectangles of shaded silky ribbon and six of white poplin ribbon. Cut the petal shapes. Crinkle by the damp cloth method and attach a length of 28-gauge white covered wire to the centre of each with adhesive.

Speckle the shaded petals with brown felt-tip pen.

Tool the edges of each petal, wire upwards, with the smooth curved foot. Tool down the wire from tip to base. Let the petals curl back naturally.

To make the Tiger Lily centre, cut seven 90mm (3⁹⁄₁₆in) lengths of 28-gauge white covered wire. Tape 20mm (1³⁄₁₆in) at one end of each wire with half-width brown stem tape. Make a small hook at the tip of each of six wires and bend the wires at right angles. Assemble the bent wires around the straight pistil wire and secure the base by the twisting method, using 30-gauge wire. Neaten with stem tape.

To make the White Lily centre, follow the same process as for the Tiger Lily, using yellow covered wire and yellow stem tape.

2 Attach the flower centre to a length of 20-gauge stem wire. Tape three petals evenly around the centre with reinforcing wires on the

outside. Tape the remaining three petals over the spaces between the first three and tape the stem. Open out the petals and the stamen centre.

3 To make an open bud, thicken the tip of a 20-gauge stem wire with brown (Tiger Lily) or yellow (White Lily) stem tape. Cut and tool six petals, as above. Tape the first three petals around the stem wire with reinforcing wires on the outside; attach the other three petals over the spaces between the first three with the wires on the inside. Curve the petals to create a natural effect. Tape to finish the stem.

4 To make a closed bud, cut six 180mm (7⅛in) lengths of 33-gauge white covered wire and tape the centre 72mm (2¹³⁄₁₆in) with white or yellow tape, according to flower colour. Narrow the taped section at top and bottom.

Cut six 24×100mm (¹⁵⁄₁₆×3¹⁵⁄₁₆in) rectangles of silky ribbon. Apply double-sided tape to one long side of each rectangle. Wrap each rectangle around a taped wire, keeping the ribbon as straight as possible and secure by the double-sided tape. Wire the six tubes together, immediately below the thickened sections by the twisting method using 30-gauge wire. Turn the tubes upside down and wire the base by the twisting method, keeping the joined edges of the tubes to the inside. Secure with tape and join in a 20-gauge stem wire. Tape to finish the stem.

Make the white bud in the same way with rectangles of white poplin ribbon. Smaller buds can be made using five, four or three tubes, which may also be shorter in length.

5 To make one leaf, cut a 12×72mm (⁷⁄₁₆×2¹³⁄₁₆in) rectangle of green silky ribbon. Fold in half and apply double-sided tape down the centre of one half. Attach a length of green covered wire to the tape and fold over the second half to line the first. Cut the leaf shape.

Make at least two leaves for each bud or flower stem.

To assemble a lily spray, attach a pair of leaves to the stem of a closed bud. Tape down the stem and join in an open bud, adding more leaves, and continue by joining in a full flower with leaves. You can select the number of buds and flowers in a spray to suit a proposed arrangement.

TULIP

MATERIALS

| Silky ribbon in white |
| Acetate ribbon in green |
| Medium-sized lily stamens |
| Stem tape in green, white and black |
| 30-gauge wire |
| 28-gauge white covered wire |
| 24-gauge green covered wire |
| 18-gauge stem wire |
| Double-sided adhesive tape in 5mm (³⁄₁₆in) and 36mm (1⁷⁄₁₆in) widths |

1 Cut twelve 45×80mm (1¹³⁄₁₆×3⅛in) rectangles from white silky ribbon. On each of six

rectangles, apply 5mm (³⁄₁₆in) double-sided tape down the centre and attach a length of white covered wire. Cover with another rectangle of white silky ribbon to line the first. Cut six petals and curve the reinforcing wires.

Tool down the centre of each petal using the smooth curved head. Then work from the base around the edge of one side, across the top and down the other side.

Wire the six petals together in double-row sequence using 30-gauge wire with the concave side of each petal facing you. Keep an even allowance of ribbon below the sequence wiring.

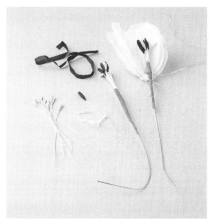

2 Cover the heads of six lily stamens with half-width black stem tape. Strengthen about half of each stamen stem by covering with half-width white stem tape.

Make a pistil by taping together three self-coloured lily stamens; do not tape the heads. Bend the heads at right angles to their stems.

Assemble the black stamens around the pistil and secure about 25mm (1in) below the stamen heads by the twisting method, using 30-gauge wire. Cover the ends of wire with half-width white stem tape. Join in an 18-gauge stem wire and tape with green stem tape.

Wrap the petals around the flower centre, with the last petal overlapping the first. Hold the ends of 30-gauge wire and twist the flowerhead to secure. Trim the wire ends and neaten with stem tape. Continue taping the stem; to imitate the fleshy tulip stem, thicken with stem tape or tissue.

3 Cut two 64×160mm (2½×6⁵⁄₁₆in) rectangles of green acetate ribbon. Cover the matt side of one with 36mm (1⁷⁄₁₆in) double-sided tape. Attach a 165mm (6½in)

length of green covered wire to the centre. Cover with the second rectangle of acetate ribbon matt side down. Cut the leaf shape.

Hairpin wire the base of the leaf with 30-gauge wire and neaten with stem tape. Attach the leaf to the base of the flower stem and secure with stem tape.

If making a tulip with dark coloured petals, use green covered wire to reinforce them. If several leaves are made, vary the sizes to create a natural effect.

WALLFLOWER (Cheiranthus)

MATERIALS
Velvet silky ribbon in dark red
Acetate ribbon in green
Yellow stamens
Stem tape in dark red and green

30-gauge wire
24-gauge green covered wire
20-gauge stem wire
5mm (³/₁₆in) double-sided adhesive tape

1 Cut four 24mm (¹⁵/₁₆in) squares of dark red velvet ribbon and shape petals. Crinkle by the spiral twist method. Wire the petals in single-row sequence, with the velvet side facing you, using one length of 30-gauge wire looped at one end.

2 Fold one stamen string in half to bring the heads together at slightly different levels. Tape the base with half-width green stem tape.

Wrap the petals around the stamen centre with the velvet side inside. Hold the ends of 30-gauge wire together and twist the flowerhead to secure. Neaten with half-width green stem tape and cover the wire ends to make a 50mm (2in) stem. Open the petals and pull them into shape.

To make a bud, fold two petals together with the velvet sides outside. Secure the base by the twisting method, using 30-gauge wire, and neaten with half-width green stem tape.

To make a closed bud, thicken the

end of a 20-gauge stem wire with dark red tape to form a bud shape. Finish with green stem tape.

Make several buds and flowers for one flower stem.

3 Cut a 24×40mm (¹⁵/₁₆×1⁹/₁₆in) rectangle of green acetate ribbon. Fold it in half and cover one half with double-sided tape. Attach a length of green covered wire to the centre of the taped half and fold over the other half to line the first. Cut the leaf shape.

Make several leaves for one flower stem.

To assemble, attach the buds, flowers and leaves to a 20-gauge stem wire using green stem tape.

WATER LILY

MATERIALS
Shaded organdy ribbon in cream/ pink
Shaded poplin ribbon in cream/pink
Poplin ribbon in green
Pointed dark-tipped stamens
Green stem tape
30-gauge wire
24-gauge green covered wire
24-gauge white covered wire

18-gauge stem wire
36mm (1⁷⁄₁₆in) double-sided adhesive tape

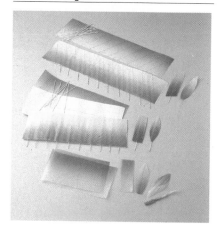

1 Cut ten 24×72mm (¹⁵⁄₁₆×2¹³⁄₁₆in) rectangles of shaded organdy ribbon and shape petals A. Crinkle by the spiral twist method.

Cut two 72×200mm (2¹³⁄₁₆×7⁷⁄₈in) rectangles of shaded poplin ribbon. Cover one piece with double-sided tape. Attach ten 80mm (3⅛in) lengths of white covered wire, evenly spaced, across the taped ribbon. Cover with the second rectangle. Cut the strip into ten pieces, each with a wire down the centre, and cut ten petals B.

Cut two 72×275mm (2¹³⁄₁₆×10⁷⁄₈in) rectangles of shaded poplin ribbon. Cover one rectangle with double-sided tape. Attach ten 90mm (3⁹⁄₁₆in) lengths of white covered wire, evenly spaced across the rectangle and slanted at an angle of about 70 degrees to the ribbon edge. Cover with the second rectangle of poplin. Cut ten petals C.

2 Wire each group of petals in double-row sequence, using 30-gauge wire. Make sure the allowance of ribbon below the wires is even.

3 Assemble thirty stamens and fold them in half. Secure the base with 30-gauge wire. Neaten with full-width green stem tape and join in an 18-gauge stem wire.

Wrap the wired petals A around the stamen centre and secure by holding the ends of 30-gauge wire and twisting the flower. Trim the wires short and neaten with stem tape. The stamens should stand about 15mm (⁹⁄₁₆in) above the petal centres.

Wrap the wired petals B around the flower and secure and tape them as above. Add the petals C, secure them and tape the base of the flower. Pull the petals back from the flower centre and gently curve inwards the reinforcing wires of the B and C petals.

4 To make the bud, cut a 72×100mm (2¹³⁄₁₆×3¹⁵⁄₁₆in) rectangle of green poplin ribbon and one of shaded poplin. Cover the green rectangle with double-sided tape and attach five 80mm (3⅛in) lengths of white covered wire evenly spaced across the rectangle. Cover with the shaded rectangle.

Repeat using two rectangles of shaded poplin ribbon. Cut five petals B from each lined rectangle, each with a wire at the centre.

Wire the bud petals in double-row sequence using 30-gauge wire, alternately one shaded and one green petal, with the green sides facing away from you.

Make a stamen centre as for the full flower and join in an 18-gauge stem wire. Wrap the bud petals around the flower centre, green sides outside, and secure by holding the ends of 30-gauge wire and twisting the bud. Trim the wires and neaten with stem tape. Curve the bud petals inwards.

5 Cut two 48mm (1⁷⁄₈in) squares of green poplin ribbon. Cover one with double-sided tape.

Cut one 75mm (3in) and six 20mm (¹³⁄₁₆in) lengths of green covered wire. Attach the long wire to the taped square across the diagonal and position three short lengths on either side to form a radiating pattern from the centre of the square. Cover with the second square of green poplin.

Cut the leaf shape and stretch the edges between the wire ends. Tape the leaf stem with half-width green stem tape. Bend the stem at right angles to the leaf.

Leaves vary in size to 72mm (2¹³⁄₁₆in) square and 96mm (3¹³⁄₁₆in) square. To make the largest leaf, it may be necessary to join ribbon sections. To do this, cut two 48×96mm (1⁷⁄₈×3¹³⁄₁₆in) rectangles and join them into one using double-sided tape to hold the edges together. Make the large leaves in the same way as the small leaf, adjusting measurements of the wires to fit the dimensions.

To make a curled leaf, roll the edges over a stem wire.

To assemble, tape the bud, flower and leaf stems together and curve the individual stems to form a base on which the water lily sits.

Flowers from Cut-out Petals

FORGET-ME-NOT
(Myosotis)

MATERIALS
Forget-me-not petals
Cold fabric dye in blue
Yellow round stamens
Green stem tape
22-gauge stem wire
Flowermaking adhesive

Dye the petals blue and allow them to dry. When dry, tool each petal with the forget-me-not head to mould the shape.

Cut the yellow stamen strings in half. Make a hole in the centre of each petal with a darning needle or length of fine wire and push a stamen through. Dab adhesive onto the petal around the hole and hold the stamen head in place for 30 seconds. Leave to dry.

Join a small group of florets with half-width green stem tape and tape them to a half-length of 22-gauge stem wire. Tape to the end of the stem.

LILAC
(Syringa)

MATERIALS
Lilac petals
White round stamens
Stem tape in green and white
22-gauge stem wire
Flowermaking adhesive

Tool each petal to curl back the sections, working from the outer tip inwards with the shiny side of the petal on the outside. Make a hole in the centre of each petal with a darning needle or piece of fine wire.

Cut the heads off the stamen strings at one end. Push a stamen through the hole in each petal. Dab adhesive onto the petal around the hole and hold the stamen head in place for 30 seconds. Leave to dry.

Make up sixty florets. Tape a quarter of each stamen stem with half-width white stem tape, then another quarter with green stem tape.

Tape six florets into a cluster with green stem tape and join in a length of 22-gauge stem wire. Work down and around the stem adding further clusters of florets and taping the wires together to form the main stem. Finish off the stem with tape.

LILY OF THE VALLEY
(Convallaria majalis)

MATERIALS
Lily of the valley petals
Acetate or silky ribbon in white
White round stamens
Green stem tape
30-gauge wire
22-gauge stem wire
Flowermaking adhesive

Tool the centre and each section of all the petals on the dull side with the small ball head. Make a small hole at the centre of each petal with a darning needle or piece of fine wire.

Cut the white stamen strings in half and push one stamen through the centre of each petal. Dab adhesive onto the petal around the hole and hold the stamen head in place for 30 seconds. Allow the adhesive to dry.

Make eight small florets in this way. Stick together the edges of the petals to close up the florets. Tape the stamen stems with half-width stem tape.

To make a bud, cover a very small piece of cotton wool with a 24mm (^{15}/16in) square of white acetate ribbon. Secure by the twisting method, using 30-gauge wire and tape with half-width green stem tape.

Use a stamen as a tiny bud and attach the buds to one end of the 22-gauge stem wire. Secure with half-width green stem tape. Trim the stem wire to half-length. Continue taping down the stem, adding in the flowers at intervals of about 15mm (^{9}/16in).

Small Filler Flowers

MATERIALS
Small scraps of silky or acetate ribbon
Stamens to tone with petal colour
Stem tape to tone with petal colour
24-gauge white covered wire
Flowermaking adhesive

Cut three 24mm (15/16in) squares of ribbon. Fold each in four and cut the floret shape. Tool with the smooth curved head from the outer sections inwards to curve the petals.

Make a hole in the centre of each floret with a darning needle or wire. Fold a stamen in half and push it through the hole. Dab adhesive onto the petal around the hole and hold the stamen heads in place for 30 seconds. Leave to dry.

Make up three florets and attach one to the end of a length of white covered wire using half-width stem tape. Add the second and third florets at intervals of about 20mm (13/16in) down the stem.

Make a number of small sprays in the same way, varying the colours of petals and stamens. You can tape several sprays together, if required, and add a heavy stem wire, depending on use. The small filler flowers are ideal for posies, headdresses, corsages and gift decorations.

You can vary the shape of the flower sprays by cutting the petal shapes differently, by tooling the petals inwards or curling them, varying the type and number of stamens at the flower centre, or arranging the stamens to stand above the petal tips.

Foliage

BAMBOO (Arundinaria)

MATERIALS
Two-colour silky ribbon in brown/ green
Acetate ribbon in green
Green stem tape
26-gauge green covered wire
16-gauge padded craft wire
36mm (1⁷/16in) double-sided adhesive tape

1 Cut two 72mm (2¹³/16in) squares of green acetate ribbon. Cover the matt side of one square with double-sided tape.

Cut twelve 72mm (2¹³/16in) lengths of green covered wire and attach them to the adhesive tape, six arranged evenly across one side of the square and six on the other. Leave about a 10mm (³/8in) gap between the wire ends across the centre of the square. Cover with the second square of green acetate, shiny side up.

Divide the ribbon square across the centre and cut six equal rectangles from each half, with a wire at the centre of each. Cut a point at top and bottom of each rectangle to form twelve leaves.

Tape 10mm (³/8in) of each leaf stem and tape them together in four groups of three. Curve each leaf back at right angles to its stem.

2 Cut four 72mm (2¹³/16in) squares of two-colour ribbon and cover one side of each with double-sided tape. Divide each square into three equal rectangles, all with the colour shading running the same way.

Tape the top of a padded craft wire with green stem tape to form a node. Attach a group of three leaves and secure with tape. Remove the backing paper from the double-sided tape on one rectangle of shaded ribbon and wrap the ribbon firmly and evenly around the padded wire, covering the bottom of the leaf stem.

Wrap another piece of ribbon around the stem, matching the colour at the join. Join in a second group of leaves, taping with half-width stem tape to form a thickened leaf joint; allow the tape to twist to get this effect. Cover the stem below this with shaded ribbon, again matching the colour to the piece above.

Work down the stem in the same way, adding all the leaf groups. Keep the ribbon seams aligned down the length of the stem. Bend the leaves slightly outwards from the main stem.

BEECH LEAVES

MATERIALS

Shaded silky ribbon in yellow/brown, or plain silky ribbon in green

Stem tape in brown or green

30- and 26-gauge covered wire in brown or green

5mm (³/₁₆in) double-sided adhesive tape

1 To make one leaf, cut a 60mm (2³/₈in) square of silky ribbon in the chosen colour. Fold in half and apply double-sided tape down the centre of one half inside the fold. Attach a 120mm (4³/₄in) length of 26-gauge covered wire to the tape and fold over the other half of the rectangle to line the first. Cut the leaf shape.

Mark the leaf veins with the tool blade head or scissor blades.

2 Cut a 40mm (1⁹/₁₆in) length of 30-gauge covered wire and tape the end with half-width stem tape to form a node. Tape the node to the base of the leaf.

For a full branch of beech leaves, make leaves of varying sizes.

Assemble leaves singly or paired and tape them together to form a

single stem. It may be necessary to join in an 18-gauge stem wire to provide enough support.

EUCALYPTUS

MATERIALS

Silky ribbon in grey/green or light brown, or acetate ribbon shaded in bronze/green

Stem tape in beige or brown

30-gauge wire

22- and 18-gauge stem wire

FOR METHOD 2

28-gauge white covered wire

5mm (³/₁₆in) double-sided adhesive tape

Method 1 Cut six 24mm (¹⁵/₁₆in) squares of silky ribbon and six 36mm (1⁷/₁₆in) squares. Cut one leaf

shape from each square and stretch between thumbs and forefingers.

Wire two small leaves together by the twisting method, using 30-gauge wire. Leave a 40mm (1⁹/₁₆in) wire stem and cover with half-width stem tape. Attach another pair of small leaves to this stem by the twisting method, leaving a 50mm (2in) stem. Tape the wire stem and add a third pair of leaves in the same way, joining in the 22-gauge stem wire before taping.

Make a second stem of three pairs of leaves and join it to the main stem to form a Y shape with the first leaf stem. Attach two larger leaves at the join.

Continue taping down the main stem, securing pairs of larger leaves at intervals, one on each side of the stem. Gently ease the leaves back from the stem.

To make a larger stem, use 18-gauge stem wire for the main stem and increase the leaf sizes as they descend.

Method 2 Cut two squares of silky ribbon for each leaf. Apply double-sided tape diagonally across the centre of one pair. Attach an 80mm (3¹/₈in) length of white covered wire to each strip of adhesive tape and cover with the second square of silky ribbon. Cut the leaf shapes.

Tape together the stems of two small leaves with half-width stem tape. Tape the stem and join in a second and third pair of leaves.

Make up a second leaf stem and join the leaf stems to a 22-gauge stem wire and continue taping, adding more pairs of leaves at intervals of about 40mm (1⁹/₁₆in). Finish off by taping to the end of the stem.

FERN

MATERIALS
Silky ribbon in green
30- and 26-gauge green covered wire
Double-sided adhesive tape in 5mm (³⁄₁₆in) and 36mm (1⁷⁄₁₆in) widths

1 Cut two 20×36mm (¹³⁄₁₆×1⁷⁄₁₆in) rectangles of green silky ribbon. Apply 36mm (1⁷⁄₁₆in) double-sided tape to one piece.

Cut six 17mm (⁵⁄₈in) lengths of 30-gauge green covered wire. Lay them on the adhesive tape in parallel lines across the rectangle. Cover with the second rectangle of silky ribbon.

Cut between the wires to shape the fronds. Fold each frond lengthwise and crinkle by the spiral twist method.

Make additional fronds according to the length of fern stem required.

2 Loop a short length of 30-gauge green covered wire around the centre of one frond. Twist the wire to secure it and bend the ends of the frond upwards.

Cut a 5×75mm (³⁄₁₆×3in) strip of silky ribbon. Apply 5mm (³⁄₁₆in) double-sided tape down the full length. Attach a 100mm (3¹⁵⁄₁₆in) length of 26-gauge green covered

wire to the adhesive tape to form a stem.

Press the wired frond to the top of the adhesive tape at the stem tip. Attach the other fronds down the stem, laid close together at right angles to the stem wire.

A larger or longer stem can be made in the same way by increasing the size of the fronds.

HELICHRYSUM

MATERIALS
Velvet silky ribbon in grey
Grey stem tape
30-gauge wire
20-gauge stem wire

1 Cut sixteen 18mm (¹¹⁄₁₆in) squares from velvet silky ribbon and cut a leaf on the diagonal of each square. Fold each leaf twice and crinkle by the spiral twist method.

Wire the base of each leaf by the twisting method using 30-gauge wire, leaving short stems of wire about 20mm (¹³⁄₁₆in) long. Tape each stem with half-width grey stem tape.

Wire two leaves to the top of a 20-gauge stem wire. Continue taping down the stem with half-width tape, adding leaves on either side of the stem at intervals of about 10-20mm (³⁄₈-¹³⁄₁₆in).

Gently flatten the leaf shapes and curve the stems outwards to create a natural effect.

HONESTY
(Lunaria)

MATERIALS
Silky ribbon in cream
Brown round stamens
Beige stem tape
30-gauge white covered wire
20-gauge stem wire
5mm (³⁄₁₆in) double-sided adhesive tape

1 Cut eighteen 36mm (1⁷⁄₁₆in) squares of cream silky ribbon.

Cut nine 150mm (5⁷⁄₈in) lengths of white covered wire and nine 120mm (4¾in) lengths of double-sided tape. Cut the adhesive tapes in half lengthwise to form narrow tape strips. Lay the white wires on nine of the tape strips and press down firmly, leaving a stem of wire at one end.

Use a coin, bottle cap or similar object to mark a circle on nine squares of silky ribbon.

Cut the heads off several stamen

PUSSY WILLOW
(Salix discolor)

strings and place one or two heads within some circles to imitate honesty seeds. Attach them to the silky ribbon with small pieces of double-sided tape.

Attach a wire around the marked circle using the adhesive tape already in place on the wire. Leave the stem section free. Cover with a second square of silky ribbon, enclosing wires and seeds. Trim and carefully stretch each circle by pulling.

Tape the stems of white wire with half-width beige stem tape. Tape one seedhead to the top of a 20-gauge stem wire and continue taping down the wire, adding other seedheads at intervals of about 30mm (1³⁄₁₆in). Tape to the end of the stem.

JAPANESE MAPLE
(Acer)

MATERIALS
Silky ribbon in wine red
Stem tape in wine red and red-brown
26-gauge red covered wire
18-gauge stem wire
5mm (³⁄₁₆in) double-sided adhesive tape

1 From wine red silky ribbon, cut twelve 60×72mm (2³⁄₈×2¹³⁄₁₆in) rectangles, four 50×65mm (2×2⁹⁄₁₆in) rectangles and eight

40mm (1⁹⁄₁₆in) squares. For each size, trace the appropriate leaf shape on half of the rectangles.

Cut an 80mm (3¹⁄₈in) length of red covered wire and four shorter lengths to fit each leaf size. Apply double-sided tape to the leaf fingers on each marked rectangle and attach the wires, the long stem wire at the centre of the leaf. Cover with the remaining squares of wine red silky ribbon.

Cut the leaf shapes and mark the leaf veins with scissor blades or the tool blade head.

2 Thicken a point near the bottom of each leaf stem with half-width wine red stem tape to form a node. Join pairs of leaves by taping the stems together just below the nodes.

Join a pair of small leaves to a medium-sized pair with red-brown stem tape. Attach an 18-gauge stem wire and continue taping, joining in a pair of large leaves. Curve all stems to create a natural effect.

Make additional stems in the same way, varying the leaf sizes, and join the leaf stems into a branch, securing with red-brown stem tape.

Maple leaves also look very effective in citrus green colouring. Use stem tape and covered wire to match the ribbon colour.

Alternatively, vary their colouring by lining the leaves with a different colour of ribbon from that which forms the upper layer.

MATERIALS
Seal ribbon in beige
Brown stem tape
30-gauge wire
18-gauge stem wire
5mm (³⁄₁₆in) double-sided adhesive tape

1 Cut eight 36mm (1⁷⁄₁₆in) squares of seal ribbon. Apply double-sided tape to one edge of each square on the wrong side. Place a square in front of you with one corner forming the base and double-sided tape on the upper right-hand side and fold down the top corner. Fold on the left side towards the centre, then fold over the right-hand side and secure with the adhesive tape. Repeat for all squares.

Gather in the base of each velvet cone by the twisting method using 30-gauge wire. Leave a wire stem of about 10mm (³⁄₈in). Neaten with half-width brown stem tape.

Thicken the top of an 18-gauge stem wire with stem tape to form a closed bud. Tape about 20mm (¹³⁄₁₆in) down the wire and join in a pussy willow bud. Secure with stem tape, making sure the back of the bud sits firmly against the main stem. Continue taping down the stem, adding pussy willow buds at intervals of 20mm (¹³⁄₁₆in). Finish off the taping and curve the stem gently.

RIBBON MEASUREMENTS

All measurements refer to 72mm ($2\frac{13}{16}$in) wide flowermaking ribbons unless otherwise stated. These quantities make the flowers as shown in the main picture of each step-by-step sequence.

AFRICAN VIOLET
Velvet silky ribbon: 100mm ($3\frac{15}{16}$in) deep purple
Flocked ribbon: 70mm ($2\frac{3}{4}$in) green

ALSTROEMERIA
Poplin ribbons: 135mm ($5\frac{5}{16}$in) deep pink/cream; 45mm ($1\frac{13}{16}$in) white
Silky ribbon: 20mm ($\frac{13}{16}$in) pale green

ARUM LILY
Acetate ribbon 144mm ($5\frac{11}{16}$in) wide: 155mm ($6\frac{1}{8}$in) white; 420mm ($16\frac{1}{2}$in) green

AZALEA
Silky ribbons: 240mm ($9\frac{1}{2}$in) orange/pink; 300mm ($11\frac{7}{8}$in) green

BELLS OF IRELAND
Silky ribbon: 1728mm (68in) cream

BIRD OF PARADISE
Silky ribbons: 50mm (2in) orange; 50mm (2in) deep pink; 250mm ($9\frac{7}{8}$in) deep blue
Acetate ribbon: 470mm ($18\frac{1}{2}$in) green

BLUEBELL
Acetate ribbons: 75mm (3in) blue; 75mm (3in) green

BRIAR ROSE
Silky ribbons: 550mm ($21\frac{3}{4}$in) white/pale pink; 100mm ($3\frac{15}{16}$in) green

BRONZE CHRYSANTHEMUM
Silky ribbons: 2775mm ($109\frac{1}{2}$in) yellow/brown; 40mm ($1\frac{9}{16}$in) green

CAMELLIA
Poplin ribbon: 250mm ($9\frac{7}{8}$in) deep pink
Acetate ribbon: 200mm ($7\frac{7}{8}$in) green
Velvet silky ribbon: 130mm ($5\frac{1}{8}$in) white

CARNATION
For the full flower
Silky ribbons: 650mm ($25\frac{5}{8}$in) pale yellow, 50mm (2in) grey/green
For the spray
720mm ($28\frac{3}{8}$in) pale yellow; 50mm (2in) grey/green

CHINESE LANTERN
Silky ribbon: 750mm ($29\frac{5}{8}$in) brown/orange

CHRISTMAS ROSE
Silky ribbons: 425mm ($16\frac{3}{4}$in) white; 350mm ($13\frac{3}{4}$in) white/pale green
Acetate ribbon: 250mm ($9\frac{7}{8}$in) green

CLEMATIS MONTANA
Silky ribbons: 145mm ($5\frac{3}{4}$in) pale pink; 585mm (23in) green

CLIVIA
Silky ribbon: 1750mm (69in) orange/white
Acetate ribbon: 440mm ($17\frac{3}{8}$in) green

CROCUS
Silky ribbons: 255mm (10in) purple; 10mm ($\frac{3}{8}$in) yellow; 60mm ($2\frac{3}{8}$in) green

CYCLAMEN
Silky ribbons: 200mm ($7\frac{7}{8}$in) cyclamen pink; 85mm ($3\frac{3}{8}$in) green
Velvet silky ribbon: 85mm ($3\frac{3}{8}$in) green

DAFFODIL
Silky ribbons: 400mm ($15\frac{3}{4}$in) green; 90mm ($3\frac{9}{16}$in) brown
For the yellow daffodil
240mm ($9\frac{1}{2}$in) yellow
For the cream daffodil
180mm (7in) cream; 50mm (2in) yellow

EASTER LILY
Acetate ribbons: 720mm ($28\frac{3}{8}$in) white; 220mm ($8\frac{3}{4}$in) green

FORSYTHIA
Silky ribbon: 505mm ($19\frac{7}{8}$in) yellow

FREESIA
Silky ribbons: 865mm ($34\frac{1}{8}$in) cream; 160mm ($6\frac{5}{16}$in) green

FUCHSIA
Silky ribbons: 90mm ($3\frac{9}{16}$in) mauve; 75mm (3in) pink
Acetate ribbon: 75mm (3in) green

GERANIUM
Silky ribbons: 330mm (13in) pale pink; 250mm ($9\frac{7}{8}$in) green

GLADIOLUS
Silky ribbons: 460mm ($18\frac{1}{8}$in) white; 360mm ($14\frac{1}{4}$in) light green

HYACINTH
Acetate ribbons: 865mm ($34\frac{1}{8}$in) blue; 160mm ($6\frac{5}{16}$in) green

HYDRANGEA
Silky ribbons: 650mm ($25\frac{5}{8}$in) wine red/pink; 200mm ($7\frac{7}{8}$in) green
Acetate ribbon: 200mm ($7\frac{7}{8}$in) green

IRIS
Silky ribbons: 540mm ($21\frac{1}{4}$in) blue; 50mm (2in) yellow; 300mm ($11\frac{7}{8}$in) green
Acetate ribbon: 300mm ($11\frac{7}{8}$in) green

LARGE ROSE
Poplin ribbon: 1300mm (51in) pink/cream
Acetate ribbon: 640mm ($25\frac{1}{4}$in) green

LENTEN ROSE
Silky ribbon: 950mm ($37\frac{1}{2}$in) wine red/mauve
Flocked ribbons: 50mm (2in) cream; 75mm (3in) yellow
Acetate ribbon: 260mm ($10\frac{1}{4}$in) green

MAGNOLIA
Velvet silky ribbon: 480mm (19in) white; 50mm (2in) green
Silky ribbon: 480mm (19in) white
Flocked ribbon: 40mm ($1\frac{9}{16}$in) yellow

MICHAELMAS DAISY
Velvet silky or flocked ribbon: 50mm (2in) wine red; 20mm ($\frac{13}{16}$in) yellow
Acetate ribbon: 30mm ($1\frac{3}{16}$in) green

MINIATURE IRIS
For the small flower
Silky ribbons: 205mm (8in) purple; 150mm ($5\frac{7}{8}$in) green
For the large flower
895mm ($35\frac{1}{4}$in) purple; 380mm (15in) green

MORNING GLORY
Silky ribbons: 395mm ($15\frac{1}{2}$in) blue/white; 75mm (3in) white; 460mm ($18\frac{1}{8}$in) green

NERINE
Silky ribbons: 390mm ($15\frac{3}{8}$in) pink; 25mm (1in) green

ORCHID
Poplin ribbon: 835mm ($32\frac{7}{8}$in) green/white

PANSY
Velvet silky ribbon: 125mm ($4\frac{15}{16}$in) yellow
Silky ribbons: 40mm ($1\frac{9}{16}$in) yellow; 100mm ($3\frac{15}{16}$in) green

PELARGONIUM
Silky ribbons: 150mm ($5\frac{7}{8}$in) pale pink; 500mm ($19\frac{3}{4}$in) green

PEONY
Poplin ribbon: 800mm ($31\frac{1}{2}$in) pink/white
Silky ribbon: 220mm ($8\frac{3}{4}$in) cream
Acetate ribbon: 465mm ($18\frac{3}{8}$in) green

PETUNIA
Silky ribbons: 850mm ($33\frac{1}{2}$in) deep pink; 425mm ($16\frac{3}{4}$in) green

POINSETTIA
For the large flower
Velvet silky ribbon: 390mm ($15\frac{3}{8}$in) bright red; 270mm ($10\frac{5}{8}$in) green
Silky ribbon: 390mm ($15\frac{3}{8}$in) bright red; 270mm ($10\frac{5}{8}$in) green
For the small flower
Velvet silky ribbon: 135mm ($5\frac{5}{16}$in) bright red; 100mm ($3\frac{15}{16}$in) green
Silky ribbon: 135mm ($5\frac{5}{16}$in) bright red: 100mm ($3\frac{15}{16}$in) green
For the metallic effect flower
Metallic shaded ribbon: 240mm ($9\frac{1}{2}$in) pink
Silky ribbon: 240mm ($9\frac{1}{2}$in) white (for lining)

POMPON DAHLIA
Acetate ribbon: 930mm ($36\frac{5}{8}$in) red; 435mm ($17\frac{1}{8}$in) green
Velvet silky ribbon: 120mm ($4\frac{3}{4}$in) yellow

POPPY
Silky ribbons: 580mm ($22\frac{7}{8}$in) bright red; 750mm ($29\frac{5}{8}$in) green

PRIMULA
Velvet silky ribbon: 110mm ($4\frac{5}{16}$in) pale pink
Acetate ribbon: 350mm ($13\frac{3}{4}$in) green

SCABIOUS
Silky ribbons: 325mm ($12\frac{7}{8}$in) pale mauve; 110mm ($4\frac{5}{16}$in) green

SCILLA
Acetate ribbons: 75mm (3in) blue; 130mm ($5\frac{1}{8}$in) green

SMALL ROSE
Silky ribbon: 580mm ($22\frac{7}{8}$in) yellow
Acetate ribbon: 180mm ($7\frac{1}{8}$in) green

SNOWDROP
Velvet silky ribbon: 30mm ($1\frac{3}{16}$in) white
Acetate ribbon: 20mm ($\frac{13}{16}$in) white
Silky ribbon: 105mm ($4\frac{1}{4}$in) green

SPIDER CHRYSANTHEMUM
Lantern ribbon: 500mm ($19\frac{3}{4}$in) golden yellow
This ribbon is 96mm ($3\frac{13}{16}$in) wide

SPIKY DAHLIA
Acetate ribbons: 920mm ($36\frac{1}{4}$in) pink; 335mm ($13\frac{1}{4}$in) green

SPRING BLOSSOM
Silky ribbons: 290mm ($11\frac{1}{2}$in) pink; 290mm ($11\frac{1}{2}$in) white; 115mm ($4\frac{1}{2}$in) green

STEPHANOTIS
Silky ribbons: 100mm ($3\frac{15}{16}$in) white; 25mm (1in) green

STOCK
Silky ribbons: 675mm ($26\frac{5}{8}$in) pink; 250mm ($9\frac{7}{8}$in) green

SWEET PEA
Silky ribbons: 205mm (8in) pink; 80mm ($3\frac{1}{8}$in) green

TIGER LILY AND WHITE LILY
For the Tiger Lily
Silky ribbons: 640mm ($25\frac{1}{4}$in) white/yellow; 290mm ($11\frac{1}{2}$in) green
For the White Lily
Silky ribbon: 144mm ($5\frac{11}{16}$in) green
Poplin ribbon: 640mm ($25\frac{1}{4}$in) white

TULIP
Silky ribbon: 960mm ($37\frac{7}{8}$in) white
Acetate ribbon: 320mm ($12\frac{5}{8}$in) green

WALLFLOWER
Velvet silky ribbon: 435mm ($17\frac{1}{8}$in) dark red
Acetate ribbon: 120mm ($4\frac{3}{4}$in) green

WATER LILY
Organdy ribbon: 290mm ($11\frac{1}{2}$in) cream/pink
Poplin ribbon: 1250mm ($49\frac{1}{4}$in) cream/pink; 390mm ($15\frac{3}{8}$in) green

BAMBOO
Silky ribbon: 170mm ($6\frac{11}{16}$in) brown/green
Acetate ribbon: 145mm ($5\frac{3}{4}$in) green

BEECH LEAVES
For autumn stem
Silky ribbon: 780mm ($30\frac{3}{4}$in) yellow/brown
For green stem
360mm ($14\frac{1}{4}$in) green

EUCALYPTUS
For Method 1
Silky ribbon: 180mm ($7\frac{1}{8}$in) grey/green
Acetate ribbon: 110mm ($4\frac{5}{16}$in) bronze/green
For Method 2
Silky ribbon: 260mm ($10\frac{1}{4}$in) light brown

FERN
Silky ribbon: 95mm ($3\frac{3}{4}$in) green

HELICHRYSUM
Velvet silky ribbon: 145mm ($5\frac{3}{4}$in) grey

HONESTY
Silky ribbon: 255mm (10in) cream

JAPANESE MAPLE
Silky ribbon: 1790mm ($70\frac{1}{2}$in) wine red

PUSSY WILLOW
Seal ribbon: 145mm ($5\frac{3}{4}$in) beige

TREE DECORATIONS
For small butterfly
Metallic shaded ribbon: 45mm ($1\frac{13}{16}$in)
Silky ribbon: 45mm ($1\frac{13}{16}$in)
For medium butterfly
Metallic shaded ribbon: 85mm ($3\frac{3}{8}$in)
Silky ribbon: 85mm ($3\frac{3}{8}$in)
For large butterfly
Metallic shaded ribbon: 130mm ($5\frac{1}{8}$in)
Silky ribbon: 130mm ($5\frac{1}{8}$in)
For lantern
Lantern ribbon: 50mm (2in)
Acetate ribbon: 48mm ($1\frac{7}{8}$in)

African Violet

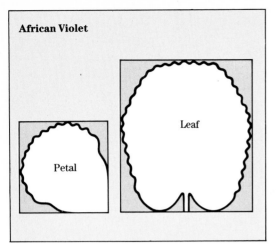

Petal

Leaf

Alstroemeria

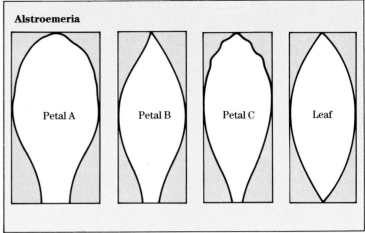

Petal A

Petal B

Petal C

Leaf

Arum Lily

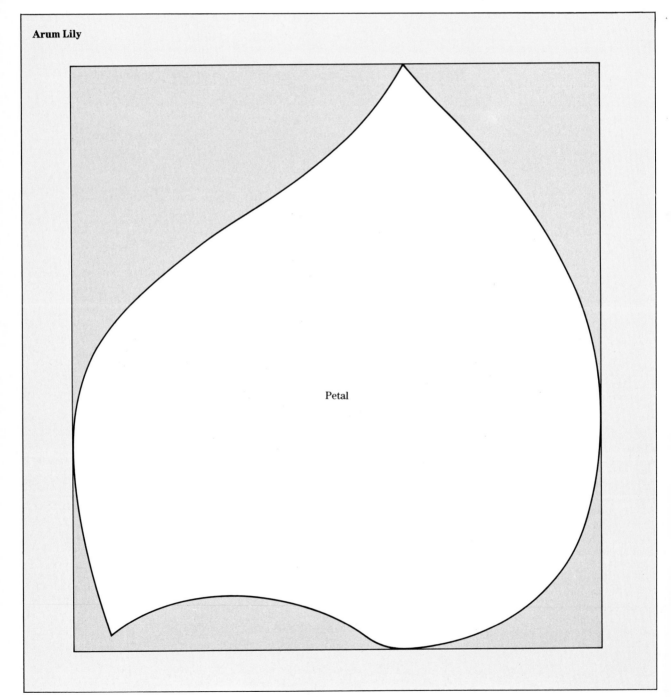

Petal

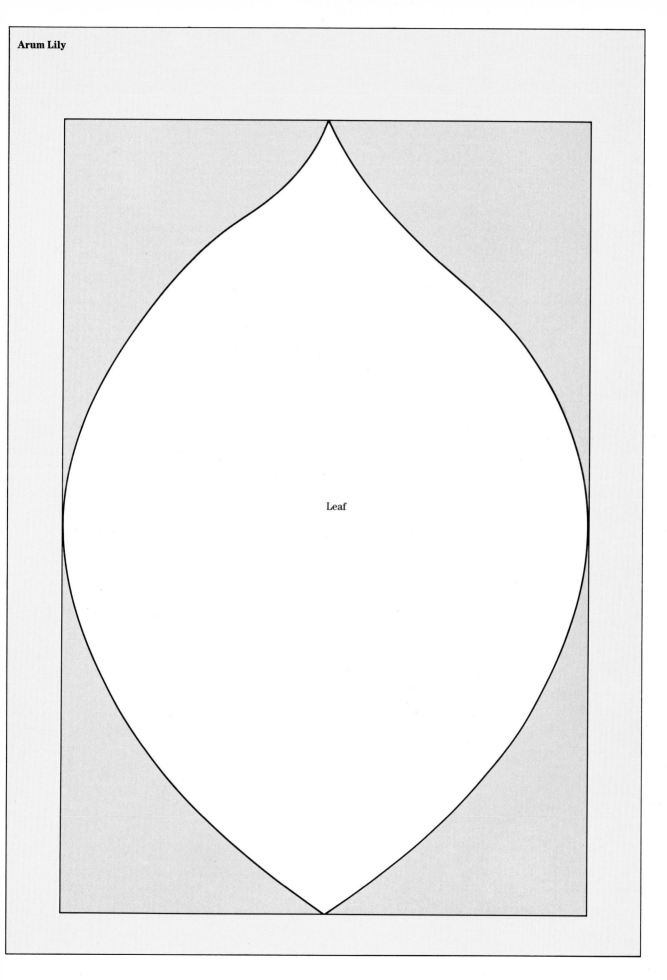

Leaf

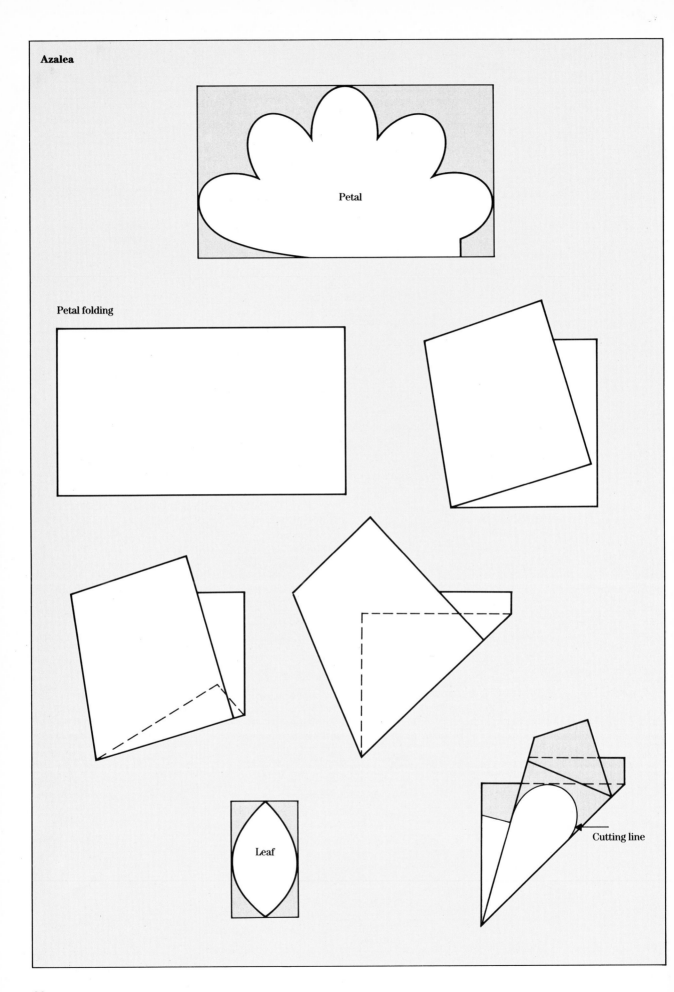

Petal

Petal folding

Leaf

Cutting line

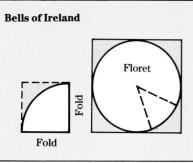

Bells of Ireland

Fold

Fold

Floret

Bluebell

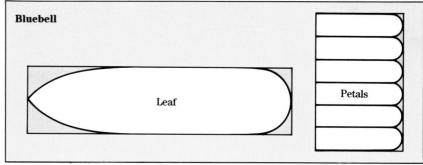

Leaf

Petals

Bird of Paradise

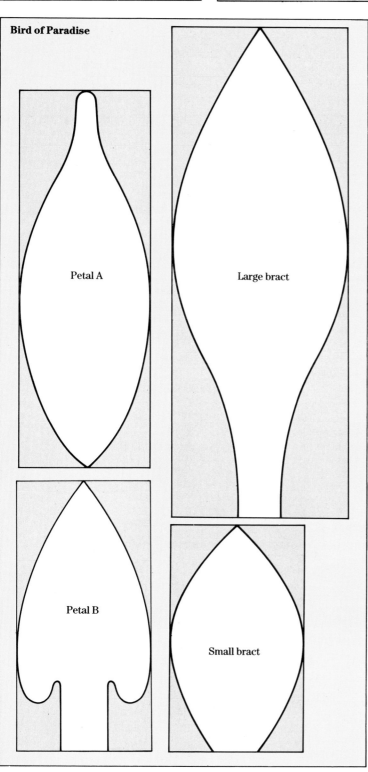

Petal A

Large bract

Petal B

Small bract

Briar Rose

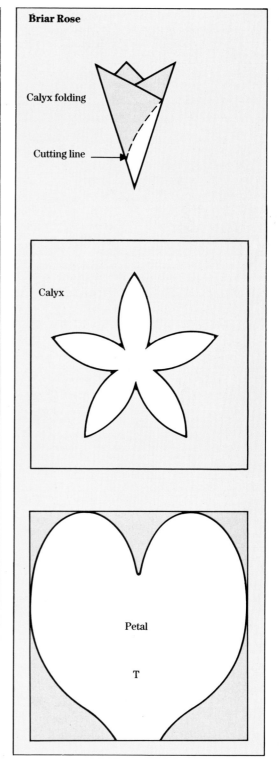

Calyx folding

Cutting line

Calyx

Petal

T

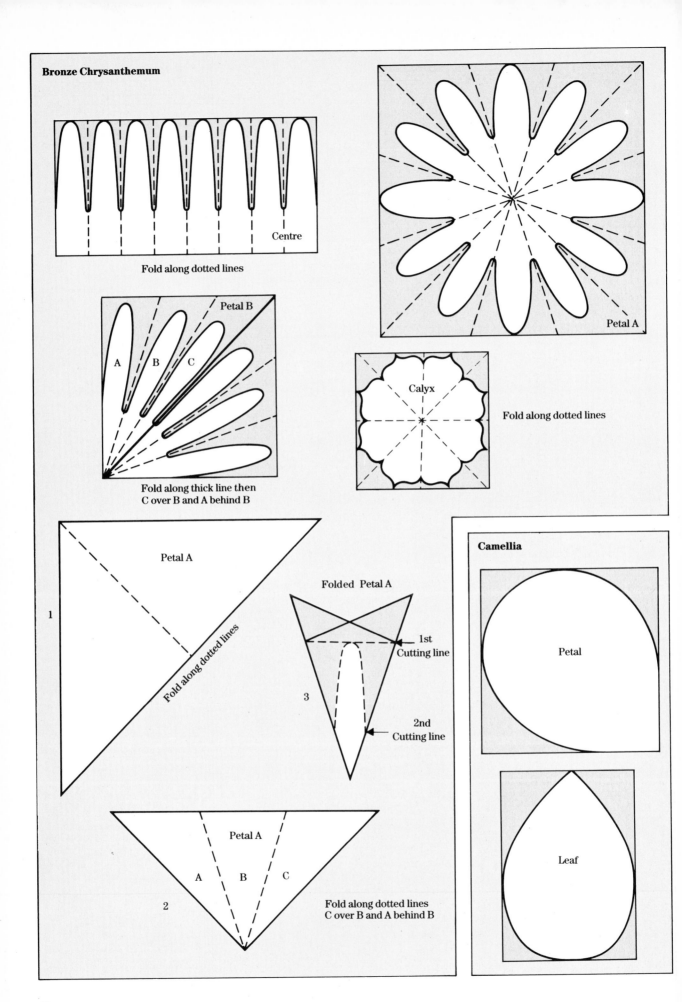

Bronze Chrysanthemum

Centre

Fold along dotted lines

Petal B

A B C

Fold along thick line then
C over B and A behind B

Petal A

Calyx

Fold along dotted lines

Petal A

1

Fold along dotted lines

Folded Petal A

1st
Cutting line

2nd
Cutting line

3

Petal A

A B C

2

Fold along dotted lines
C over B and A behind B

Camellia

Petal

Leaf

Carnation

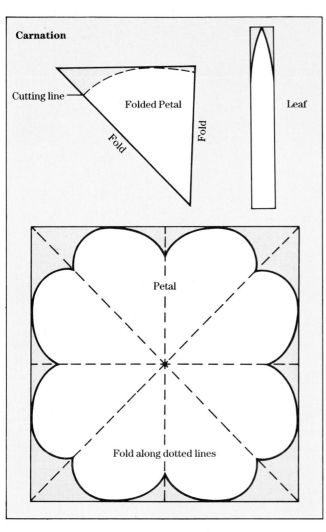

Cutting line

Folded Petal

Fold

Fold

Leaf

Petal

Fold along dotted lines

Clematis Montana

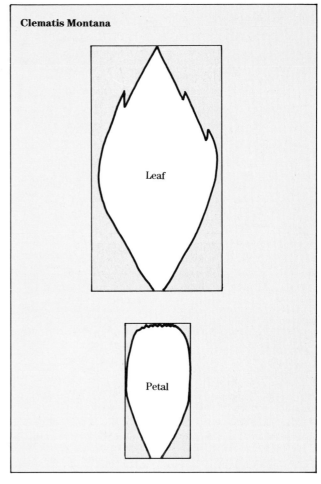

Leaf

Petal

Chinese Lantern

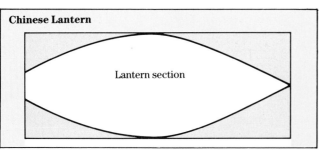

Lantern section

Christmas Rose

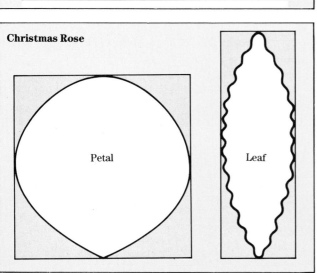

Petal

Leaf

Clivia

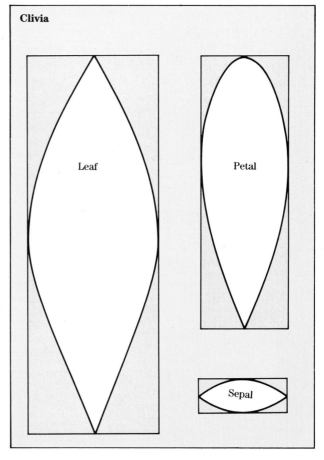

Leaf

Petal

Sepal

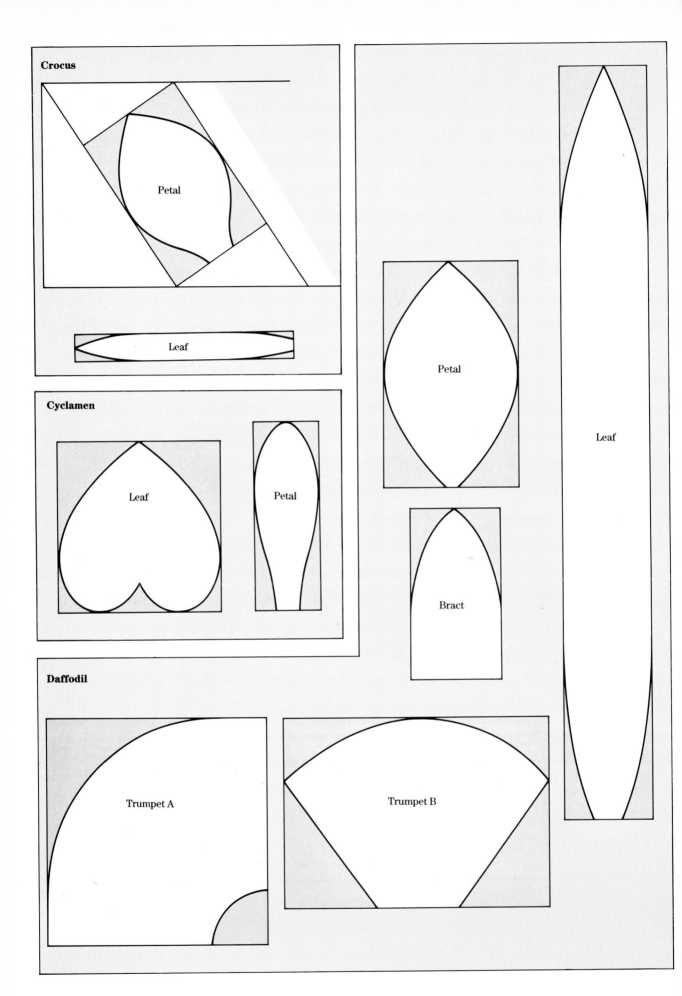

Crocus

Petal

Leaf

Cyclamen

Leaf

Petal

Petal

Bract

Leaf

Daffodil

Trumpet A

Trumpet B

70

Easter Lily

Petal

Leaf

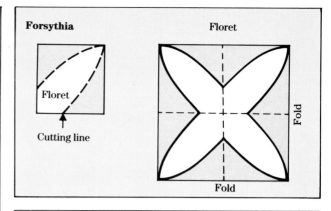

Forsythia

Floret

Floret

Cutting line

Fold

Fold

Fuchsia

Outer petal

Inner petal

Leaf

Freesia

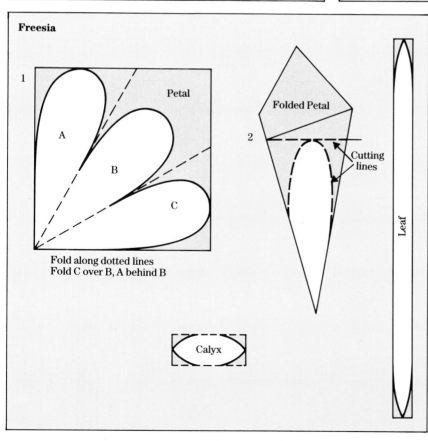

1

Petal

A

B

C

Fold along dotted lines
Fold C over B, A behind B

2

Folded Petal

Cutting lines

Leaf

Calyx

Geranium

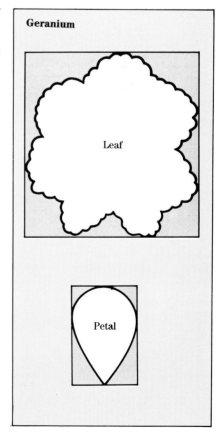

Leaf

Petal

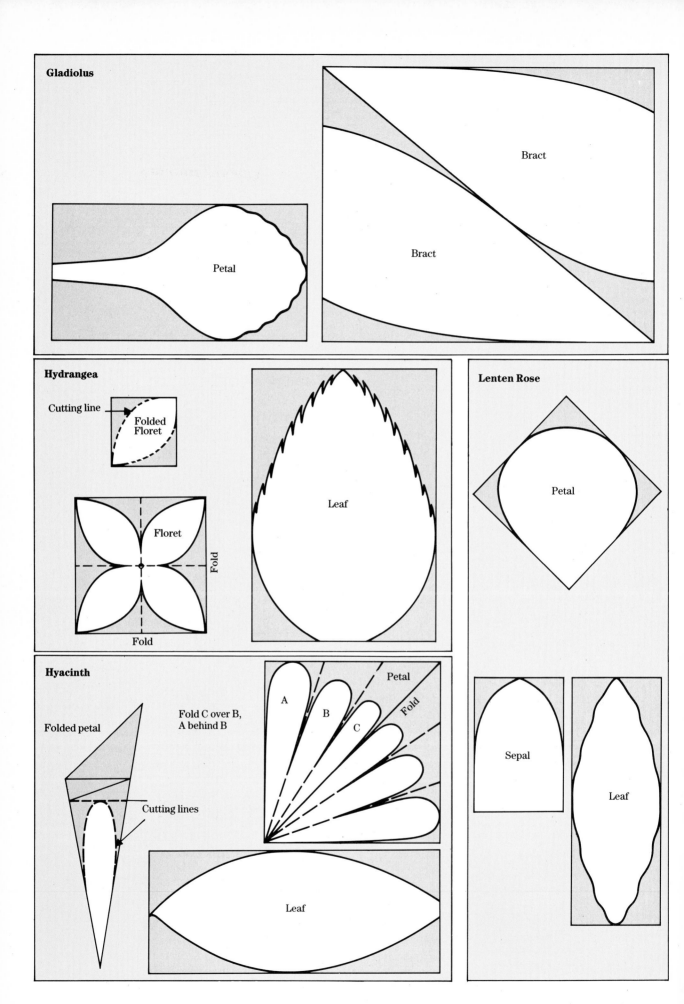

Gladiolus

Petal

Bract

Bract

Hydrangea

Cutting line →

Folded
Floret

Floret

Fold

Fold

Leaf

Lenten Rose

Petal

Hyacinth

Folded petal

Fold C over B,
A behind B

Cutting lines

A

B

C

Petal

Fold

Leaf

Sepal

Leaf

Leaf

Iris

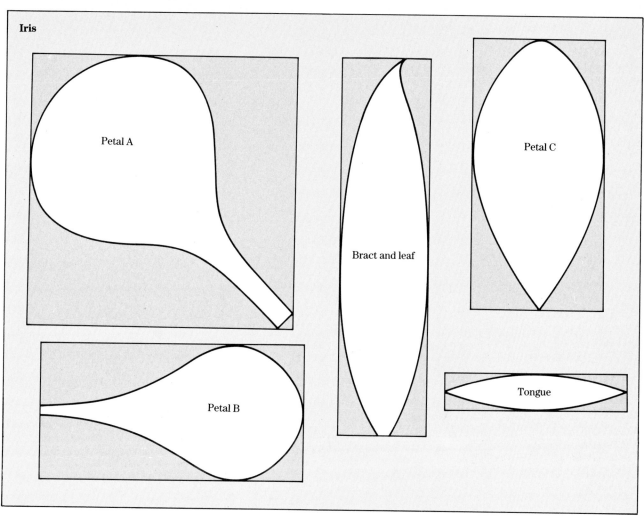

Petal A

Bract and leaf

Petal C

Petal B

Tongue

Miniature Iris

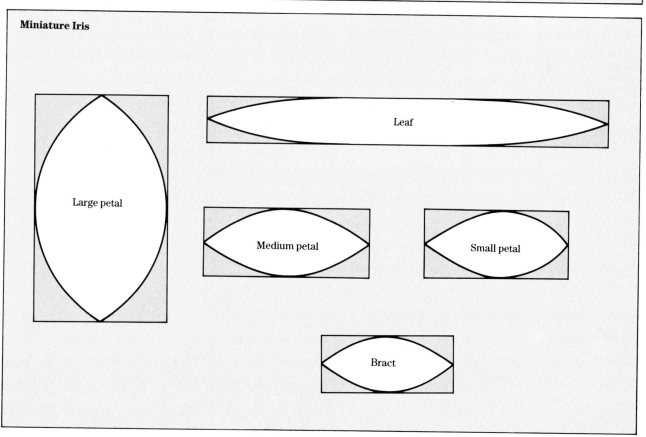

Large petal

Leaf

Medium petal

Small petal

Bract

73

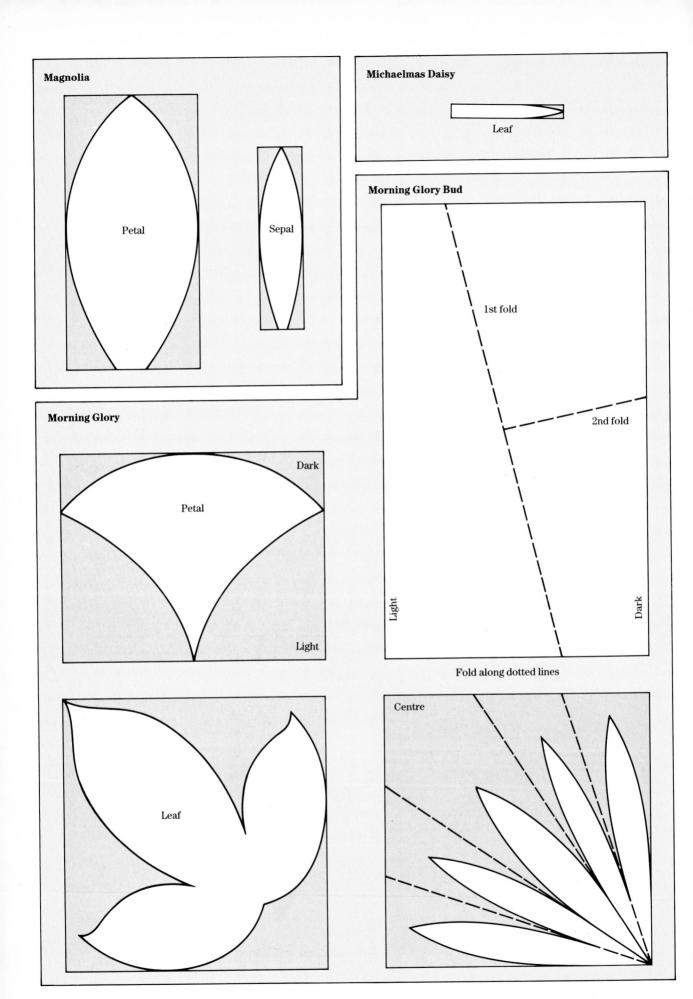

Magnolia

Petal

Sepal

Michaelmas Daisy

Leaf

Morning Glory Bud

1st fold

2nd fold

Light

Dark

Fold along dotted lines

Morning Glory

Petal

Dark

Light

Leaf

Centre

74

Nerine

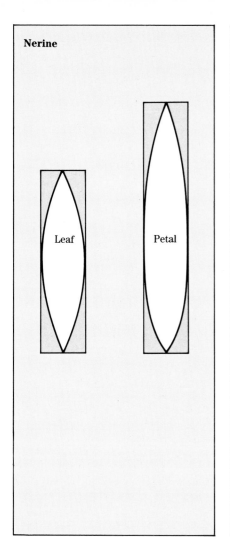

Leaf

Petal

Orchid

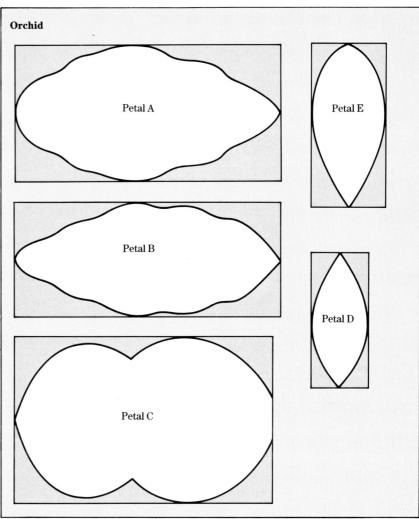

Petal A

Petal E

Petal B

Petal D

Petal C

Pansy

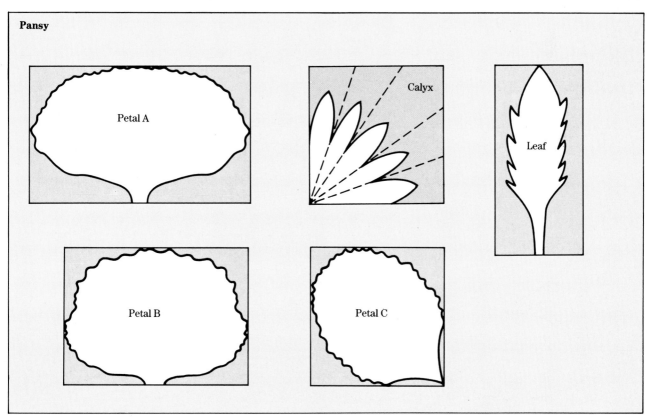

Petal A

Calyx

Leaf

Petal B

Petal C

75

Pelargonium

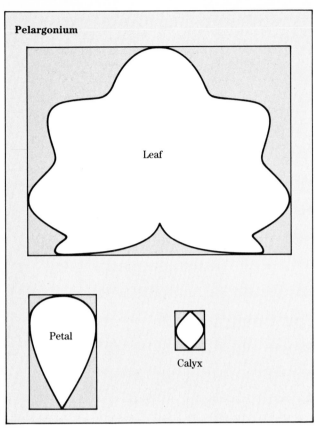

Leaf

Petal

Calyx

Peony

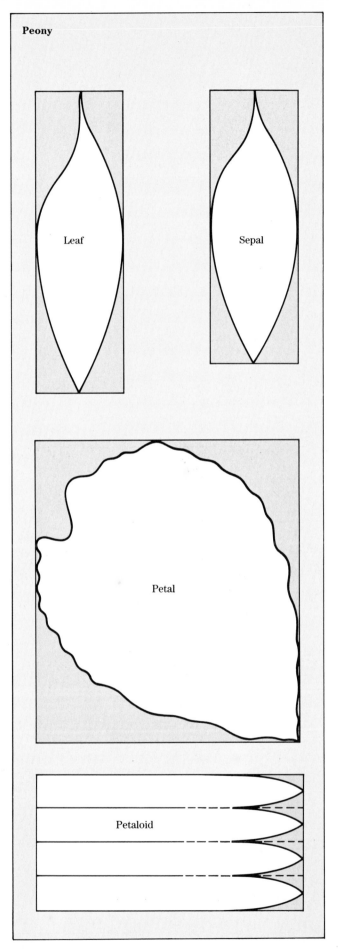

Leaf

Sepal

Petal

Petaloid

Petunia

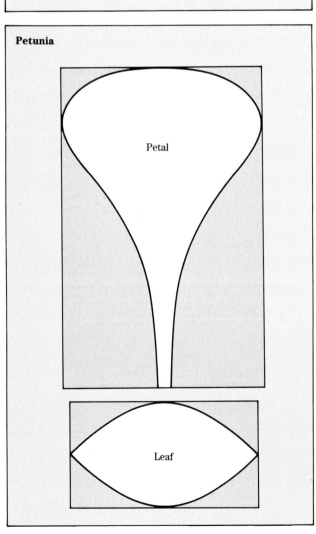

Petal

Leaf

Pompon Dahlia

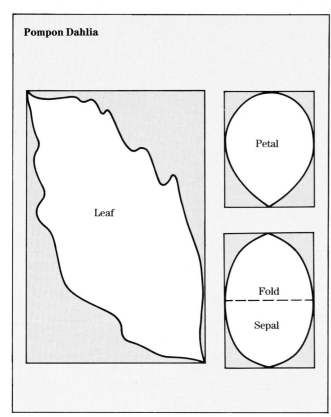

Leaf

Petal

Fold

Sepal

Primula

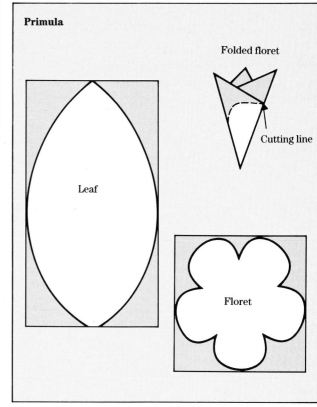

Leaf

Folded floret

Cutting line

Floret

Poppy

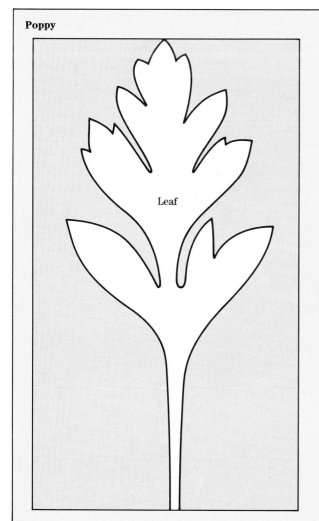

Leaf

Poinsettia

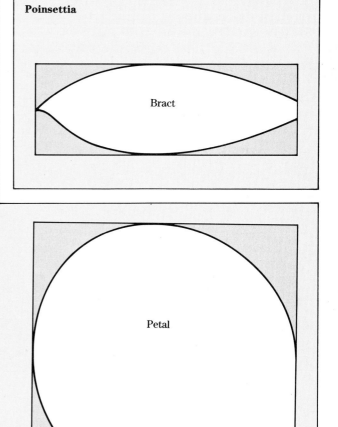

Bract

Petal

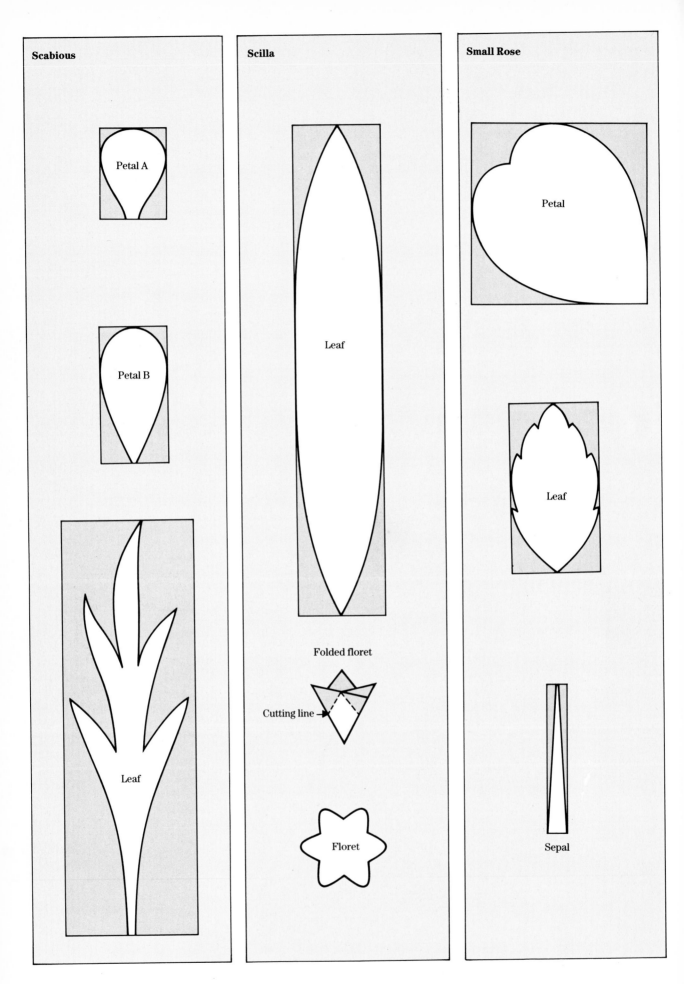

Scabious

Petal A

Petal B

Leaf

Scilla

Leaf

Folded floret

Cutting line →

Floret

Small Rose

Petal

Leaf

Sepal

78

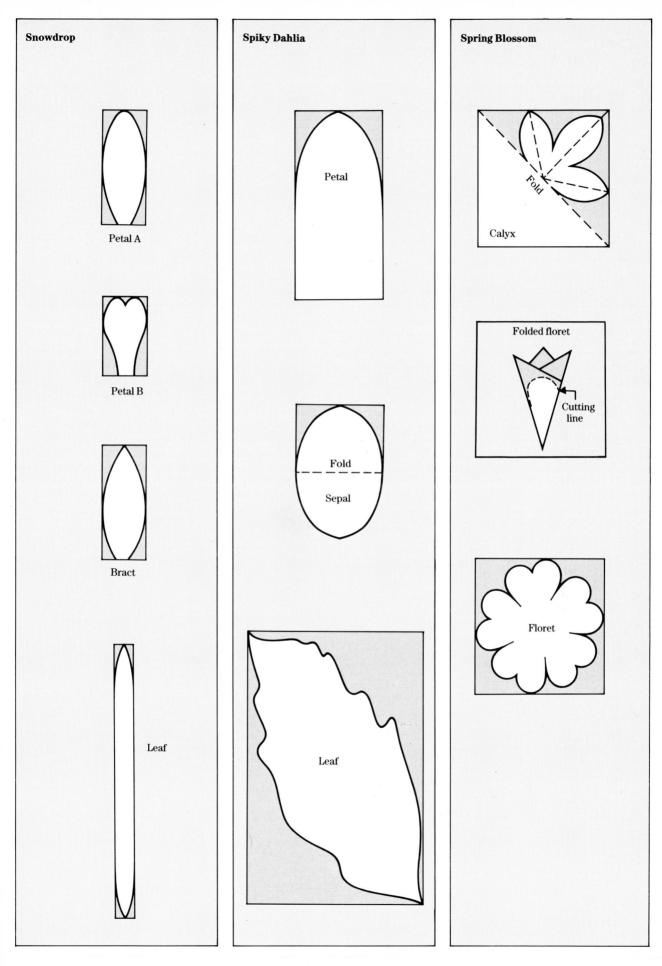

Snowdrop

Petal A

Petal B

Bract

Leaf

Spiky Dahlia

Petal

Fold

Sepal

Leaf

Spring Blossom

Fold

Calyx

Folded floret

Cutting line

Floret

79

Stephanotis

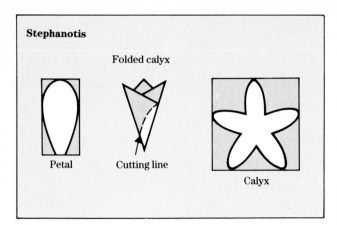

Sweet Pea

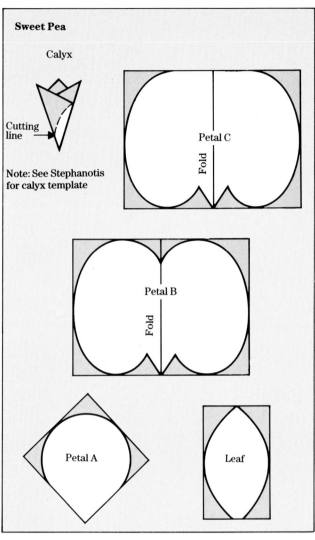

Stock

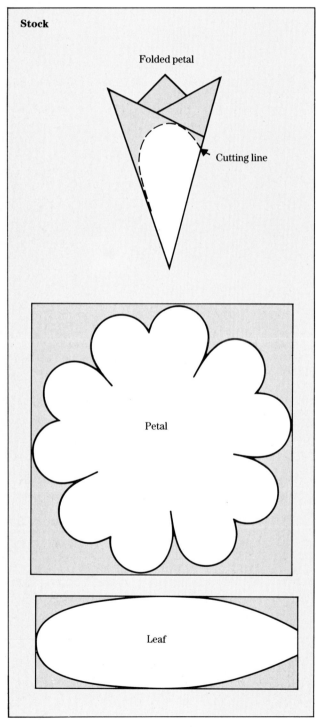

Tiger Lily and White Lily

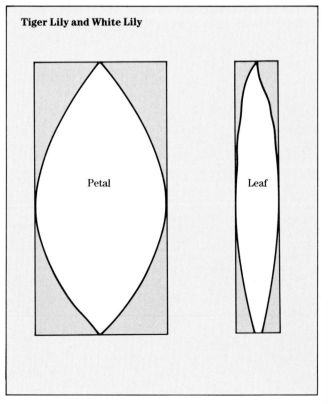

Tulip

Wallflower

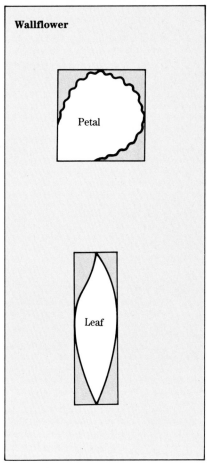

Petal

Leaf

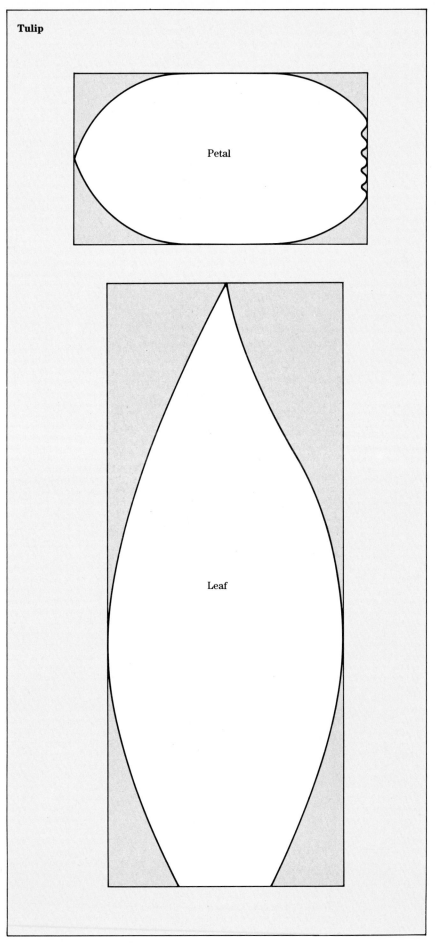

Petal

Leaf

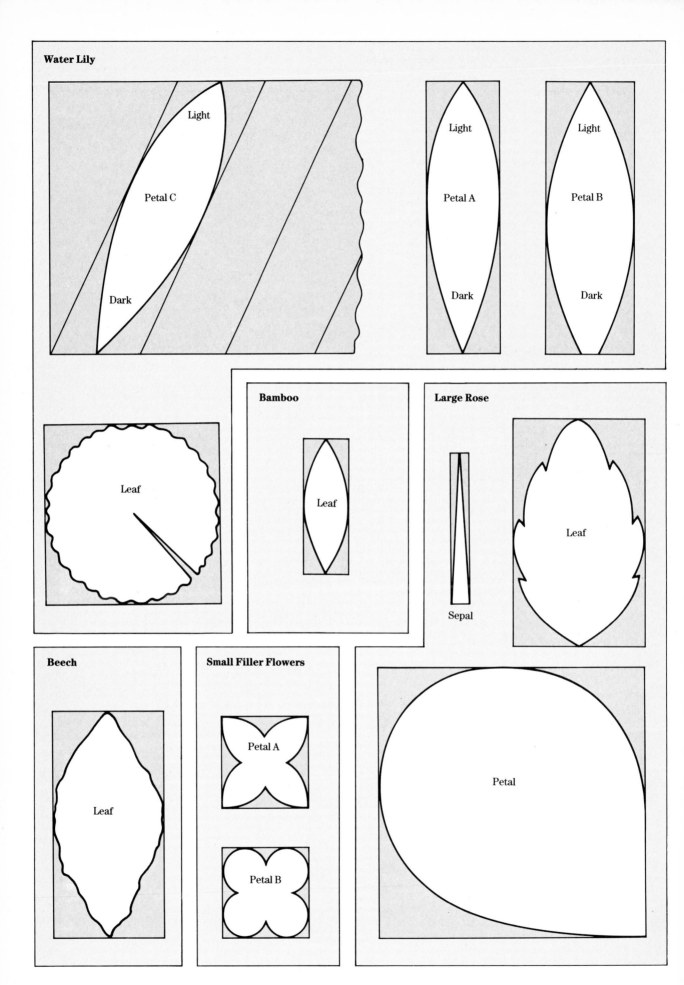

Water Lily

Light

Petal C

Dark

Light

Petal A

Dark

Light

Petal B

Dark

Leaf

Bamboo

Leaf

Large Rose

Sepal

Leaf

Beech

Leaf

Small Filler Flowers

Petal A

Petal B

Petal

82

Eucalyptus

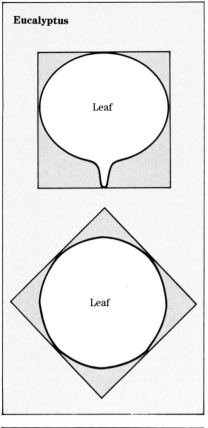

Leaf

Leaf

Japanese Maple

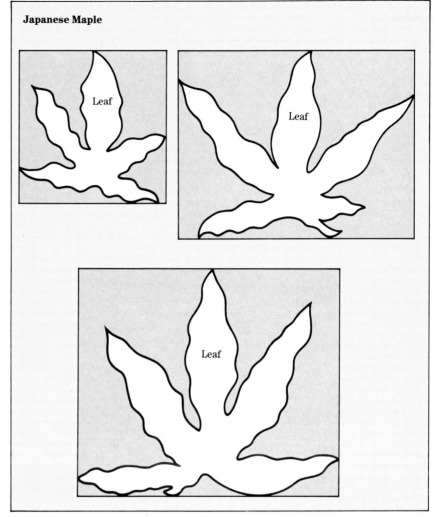

Leaf

Leaf

Leaf

Fern

Frond

Helichrysum

Leaf

Honesty

Pussy Willow

Fold as shown and roll to make bud

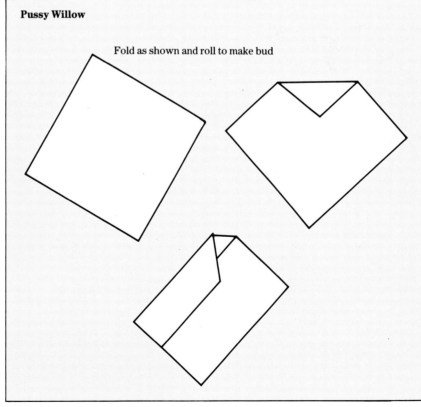

Flower Arranging with Silk Flowers

The art of arranging silk flowers follows many of the methods and design principles developed over the years for flower arranging using fresh materials. The silk-flower arranger has one distinct advantage, in that the flowers do not require a supply of water; this affects not only the permanency of the arrangement but also the way in which the materials can be placed and secured, and the types of containers and bases which can be used to support the arrangement. In addition, some fresh materials, such as the Japanese maple, cannot be maintained in good condition once cut; the silk flower arranger can make effective use of this lovely foliage in artificial form and the arrangement will last for an indefinite period.

Bases and containers

A base is not an essential component of a flower arrangement but may be used to protect the piece of furniture on which the arrangement stands or to provide visual balance to the design, creating an appropriate finishing touch.

A base of slate or a cross-cut of wood can be used with no visible container, the arrangement materials being secured directly to the base. It provides a platform to work from with regard to the height, width and depth of the arrangement and can also contribute to the atmosphere of the design; for example, to make a naturalistic setting for a landscape theme.

A useful base for a formal arrangement can be made by covering a cake-board with velvet, or for less formal styling, with a sturdy fabric such as hessian. Polished or unpolished wood, cork, bamboo, clear plastic sheets or blocks such as perspex (plexiglass), or polished marble are all excellent and versatile materials for bases.

Types of containers

Container is the term for the vase, bowl or other receptacle which holds the flowers. For silk-flower arranging the container need not be watertight so the choice is limitless, ranging from a tiny shell for a miniature arrangement to a large stone urn for a church decoration.

A container which is visible must be an integral part of the design harmonizing well with the flowers and foliages. If concealed, it is merely a means of anchoring the plant material and need only be of the appropriate shape and depth.

The container must be suitable for the shape and style of the arrangement and for the setting – an antique silver candlestick, for example, is not appropriate for a cottage kitchen, whereas an earthenware jug complements the atmosphere of the room. In fresh-flower arranging, the water in the container gives weight: silk-flower arrangements tend to be somewhat top-heavy, so the container should be broadly based or made of a weighty material, or weighted by the insertion of sand or stones.

BASKETS Being made of natural plant material, often willow, baskets have natural affinity with flowers and leaves. The interesting textures of basketwork and soft muted colours blend especially well with spring colours or the rich, vibrant hues associated with autumn. Baskets are also particularly well suited to informal settings and country-style furnishings.

METALS Brass, copper, silver and pewter are available in the form of antique kitchen utensils, plates, jelly pans and pots, as well as larger vases and urns. Brass is an excellent complement to yellows and oranges, copper to peaches and purples, pewter or silver to pinks and greys. Wrought ironwork can also add its own distinctive aesthetic value to an arrangement.

GLASS This is an ideal and attractive material for silk-flower arranging, by contrast with fresh-flower arranging, where there is the problem of the water supply producing unsightly marks on the glass. Anything from goblets and wine glasses to clear or coloured glass bowls, a builder's glass brick or a sophisticated modern glass sculpture can be used as a container for fabric flowers.

CERAMICS Old earthenware jars, ornate china, glazed vases, ovenware, hand-thrown pottery and even clay drainage pipes are all useful flower containers in the correct setting. Antique shops and junk stalls are an excellent source of patterned and glazed ceramic containers – you may even find a huge Victorian wash basin or soup tureen that would be ideal for a large massed arrangement, or a pretty piece of Dresden for a special occasion. The choice of containers is infinite, whether you buy from a department store, market stall or craft gallery.

Mechanics

This is the collective term for the various means of supporting flowers in the container. The mechanics must be firm and inconspicuous; this is particularly important in the arranging of fabric flowers, as the long stems can be heavy.

FLORISTS' FOAM There are two types of foam, one used in dry form and the type commonly used by florists and flower arrangers which can be wetted to maintain fresh plant materials. For an arrangement using fabric or preserved materials only, you will require the dry foam. It can be cut to shape and wedged into a container or anchored to other forms of mechanics. The flower or foliage stems are pushed into the hard, spongey material which will maintain them at the correct angle. The wetted foam is used in the same way when fresh materials form part of the arrangement.

Foam is available in rounds or blocks of various sizes. The size of the piece of foam used in an arrangement is important: if it is too large it is conspicuous; if too small, it falls to pieces. The correct sizing will be learned by experience.

Light stems stay where placed in the foam but long or heavy stems tend to swivel. This can be avoided by slitting the tape which binds a multi-wired stem and separating the wires into a fork which is pushed into the foam. For a single-wire stem, an extra wire is twisted around the base of the stem to form an extra 'leg'.

FIXERS AND MODELLING COMPOUNDS For anchoring plastic frogs and other forms of mechanics, you need an adhesive material which will stick to any surface and keep the mechanics firmly in place. Proprietary brand fixers such as Oasis Fix may be available, or a non-drying modelling compound, such as Plasticene, can also be used. Adhesive tapes can be useful: special tape is available for securing foam and the double-sided tape used for making the flowers may also come in handy for arranging them.

A modelling compound which dries on exposure to the air can be used as the mechanics for an arrangement. The flower stems are pressed into the compound while it is still moist and will be held firmly as it dries. This type of material can also be impaled on an anchoring device (see below) and is useful for providing extra weight in tall or narrow-based containers.

PLASTIC FROGS AND FOAM ANCHORS A frog is specially designed to support a piece of foam. It is a circle of plastic with several upright prongs on which the foam is impaled. The foam anchor, a heavy metal base with long, widely spaced pins, works in the same way.

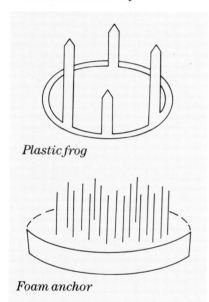

Plastic frog

Foam anchor

A frog or foam anchor needs to be fixed to the container or base, which can be done by pressing pieces of fixer or modelling compound onto the bottom of the frog or anchor and pressing this down firmly on the container or base. The container, fixer, anchor and your fingers must all be clean, dry and dust-free (especially of dust created by the florists' foam). A small piece of foam can then be impaled on the anchor and taped in place for additional security.

PINHOLDERS A pinholder has pins rising from a weighted base; a well pinholder is a small container with vertical pins inside. Pinholders are not suitable mechanics if only fabric flowers are being arranged: normally, the stems of fresh flowers are pressed onto or between the

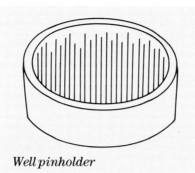

Well pinholder

pins and this is ineffective for wire stems. However, pinholders are helpful when combining fresh and fabric flowers, including natural and dried foliages with heavy stems. To support the wire stems of the silk flowers, attach a small piece of foam over the pins on part of the pinholder.

Concealing mechanics
In a traditional-style arrangement, large flowers or leaves and trailing stems can be arranged near the rim of the container to conceal the mechanics. Reindeer moss soaked until it is soft and pliable can be used for covering a foam block. It should be placed over the foam before the flowers are inserted. Garden moss, driftwood or bulb fibre could be used in a landscape arrangement or open, low container, or materials such as aquarium gravel, stones or pebbles.

Where it is inappropriate to cover the mechanics with a loose or fibrous material, the foam can be coloured with paint from an aerosol

spray can, in a colour to match the container. This is a useful method for free-form arrangements.

Basic equipment and materials
In addition to the special equipment for flower arranging, you need a pair of sharp, strong scissors capable of cutting fine wire; wire cutters for cutting heavier wires; a knife to cut the dry foam; and a supply of extra stem wires and stem tape, as used in making the fabric flowers, for lengthening or joining stems as necessary.

Checklist of equipment and materials
Scissors
Wire cutters
Knife
Florists' foam
Non-drying and drying modelling compounds
Adhesive tape
Plastic frogs and foam anchors
Well pinholders
Stem wire
Stem tape
Sand or stones for weighting containers

Preserving plant materials
In some of the arrangements shown in the following pages, dried and glycerined plant materials have been included. It is useful to acquire the skills of drying and preserving fresh materials, along with the ability to make fabric flowers, as preserved items can often supply an appropriate accent of texture or colour in a flower design.

To secure a plastic frog or foam anchor to a container, press modelling compound or fixer on to the base and press this firmly down on the container.

Foam placed on a plastic frog or foam anchor may be taped in place for additional security.

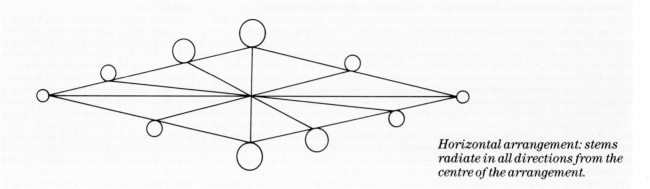

Horizontal arrangement: stems radiate in all directions from the centre of the arrangement.

Air drying
Materials such as poppy seedheads and grasses should be gathered when they are in mature condition, on a dry day. Hang them upside down in an airy, warm room until they have dried out completely.

Pressing
Large materials such as rhododendron leaves are dried by placing them between the pages of a magazine and allowing them to dry out slowly. To curve and form them, the dried leaves can be softened in steam and held in the required shape until cool – this takes about 30 seconds.

Glycerining
A solution of glycerine for preserving plant materials is made with one part glycerine to two parts boiling water. Stir the mixture well and pour it into a transparent jar, to a depth of about 50mm (2in). Trim the stems of the plant material and place them in the glycerine, leaving them until the leaf colour changes. The time taken varies with the type of foliage and the temperature of the room.

The glycerine solution should be topped up as it is taken by the leaves so that the stem ends are not allowed to dry out. Remove the material from the solution before the glycerine begins to 'sweat' from the leaves. If the stem ends tend to droop when the glycerine has been absorbed, hang the stems upside down for a few days.

The colour change varies from the creamy tones of *Choisya ternata* and *Buxus* (Box) to the dark glossy brown of *Mahonia* and the black of *Prunus Laurocerasus* (Common Laurel). To lighten the colour, hang the stems in strong sunlight for a few days.

Unblemished leaves and branches should be cut when mature, before the leaves have begun to take on autumn colours. Evergreens can be treated throughout the year.

Store glycerined materials in boxes, not in polythene bags, in a dry place not exposed to frost. Dusty leaves can be washed in warm soapy water but must be dried thoroughly before storing.

Foliages for Preserving
Beech
Butcher's Broom
Box
Choisya
Eucalyptus
Laurel
Mahonia
Pittosporum
Pussy Willow

Style and design in silk flower arranging
Flower arranging has changed and developed over centuries, from the simple basket of flowers depicted in a Roman mosaic through the symbolic Madonna Lily appearing so often in early Renaissance paintings and the mass dried bouquets beloved of eighteenth-century American Colonial styling, to the great variety of styles we recognize today.

There are six basic categories of style in flower arrangement but in each of these the use of scale, colour and texture provides an immense variation. The design elements and principles explained here are all illustrated in different ways in the specially created silk flower arrangements which follow this chapter.

Line arrangements
VERTICAL This type of arrangement has a strong upward movement and may be a tall, narrow triangle or a simple line of flowers about twice the height of the container. Often flowers with bold shapes are used, such as iris, arum lily or bird of paradise flowers. The stems of a vertical arrangement originate from a central point.
(See pages 105, 107 and 111.)
HORIZONTAL In these arrangements width becomes the main linear feature and this style is often used for table or windowsill decoration. The focal point is towards the centre and stems radiate in all directions from this area.
(See page 131.)

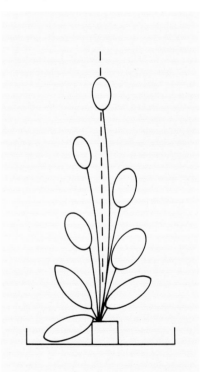

Vertical arrangement: stems originate from a central point at the base of the arrangement.

Triangular arrangements
Typical of this style is the traditional massed arrangement where there is a clear triangular outline but flowers and foliage are closely packed within this, leaving little internal space. The triangular shape may be equally balanced on each side, or asymmetrical with one point of the triangle extending further than the other.

A variety of size, shape and texture in the flowers is used. Stems radiate from a central point, usually with paler and smaller flowers at the outer edges graduating to larger, deep-coloured blooms at the centre, the point of focal interest. All components – the container, flowers, foliage and setting – should contribute to a harmonious effect.

The height of the arrangement should be about one-and-a-half times the height or width of the container (whichever is the greater) and the sides about two-thirds of this length.
(See pages 96, 101, 124, 127, 129, 130 and 136.)

Crescent arrangements
The crescent may be symmetrical or asymmetrical, the focal point being created at the base of the main stems.

A stemmed container such as a candlestick or figurine provides an elegant base for an inverted crescent or a double curve in the form of an S-shape, known as the Hogarth curve. As with the traditional triangular arrangement, increasing weight and darker colour

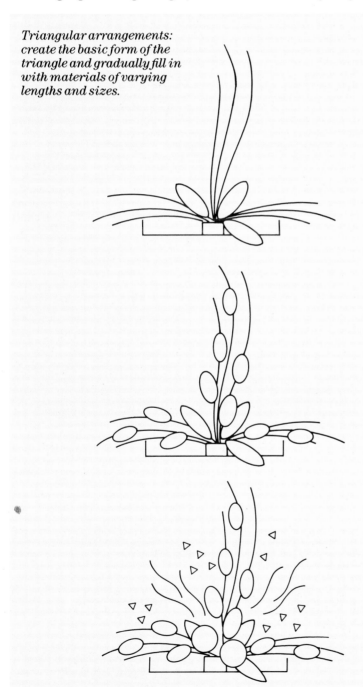

Triangular arrangements: create the basic form of the triangle and gradually fill in with materials of varying lengths and sizes.

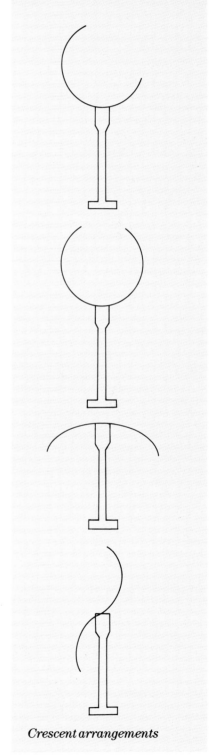

Crescent arrangements

towards the centre of the design gives a balanced and rhythmic effect.

The more complex curved shapes are easily achieved with silk flowers, as the wire stems can be bent into any shape. Smooth curves are obtained by gentle pressure of thumbs and forefingers along the wire. Avoid making angular bends in the stems, as these have an unnatural appearance.
(See pages 97, 103 and 118.)

All-round arrangements
This is the description of arrangements in which there is a circular or oval outline and a balanced and similar appearance from all sides. All stems should appear to radiate from a central point. A formal table centrepiece which will be seen from all sides should be designed in this way.
(See pages 99 and 131.)

Landscape designs
Landscape is the term applied to arrangements which represent a natural setting, such as the countryside, the seashore, moorland or a garden. A base of slate or unpolished wood is often used with the container hidden from view. Scale is of the utmost importance and simplicity and restraint in the choice of flower and foliage materials are essential.
(See page 95.)

Modern or free-form design
These designs are much influenced by Oriental styling in the economy of material and use of space. Stems radiate from a central point and the outline is strong and interesting, giving a sculptured effect. Only the minimum of material necessary to the design should be used. The effectiveness of the design often relies on contrasts of texture, form and colour.
(See pages 104 and 106.)

Elements and principles of design
To create a pleasing arrangement, it is first necessary to understand a few elements and principles of design. These are common to all visual arts and fundamental to good design of any kind.

Design elements
All natural plant material has colour, texture and shape. The skill of the flower arranger is to combine these into a harmonious design. The silk-flower arranger, not dependent on the availability of natural plant materials, can when making the flowers create all these qualities, subject only to the limits of the imagination.

With fabric flowers, the arranger can select from an almost unlimited colour range in the ribbons, with endless variation of tints, tones and shades. Strong hues can be combined with muted colours and subtle gradations from dark to light and from one colour to another can be introduced.

Flowers can be made in colours which are true to nature or divorced from nature; the silk-flower arranger can create the blue rose which has so long been the dream of rose growers.

In addition to the colour range, there are different textures in the ribbons – soft, delicate silky ribbons, stronger acetate displaying the shiny or matt surface and the rich lustrous texture of flocked and velvet ribbons, which also contribute glossy or dulled surface texture.

Colour
Colour is the most emotive of the elements. We are surrounded by colour in the home, garden and countryside, and through fashion, graphics and environmental design. Colour sense is developed through an awareness of the colours around us and with practice and experience, the arranger learns which colour combinations to use.

Looking into a real flower helps both in the making of its silk counterpart and in deciding the colours for an arrangement. Study the colour of the petals inside and out, at the edges and the base of the petals, and also the colours of the pistil and stamens; look at the contrasts and harmonies of these with the colours of the stem and both sides of the leaves. A pink tulip, for example, has purple and blue shading towards the petal bases, and blue-black stamens; hence pink blends well with these colours in an arrangement. Natural flower colours can also help with more subtle combinations of blues, greens and mauves, for example.

Some arrangers prefer the sharp contrasts of complementary or opposite colours; others prefer muted tints, tones and shades. Colour is not finite but relative to light and the proximity and density of other neighbouring colours. This is an important consideration: the background colours of walls, carpets and soft furnishings must be taken into account as the setting for an arrangement.

Colours can also be warm or cold. Oranges and reds, being associated with sunshine and firelight, are considered to be warm colours, while blue, white, grey and some greens, colours of ice and sea, are considered to be cool. These points should be considered when you are creating and positioning an arrangement because they tend to influence an atmosphere or mood;

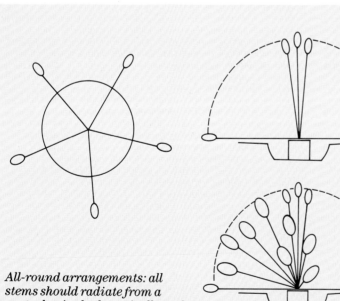

All-round arrangements: all stems should radiate from a central point both vertically and horizontally.

for example, warm colours in a hallway are welcoming.

Colour advances and recedes, according to brightness and apparent temperature. Warm or pale colours tend to advance – another reason for placing reds, oranges and yellows in a dark hallway. It should be borne in mind when creating wedding or church arrangements which may be seen from a distance that blue recedes.

Neutralized colours, those weak in hue, are a good choice for containers, because they set off the flowers. A good example of this is the beige and brown tones of basketwork. Containers in bright colours can be very dramatic but are often too eye-catching and detract from the arrangement itself. This can be avoided by repeating the container colour in the flowers. A pure white container is a dominant element but the addition of some white flowers to the arrangement creates a balancing link.

Repetition of colours creates rhythm, as does the placement of lighter colours on the outer edges of an arrangement and darker, stronger colours towards the centre.

Texture
All surfaces have a texture. It is primarily a tactile quality but we learn through experience to associate the way the texture feels with its appearance. Flower arrangers deal with surface texture in terms of rough or smooth, silky or velvety, dull or shiny. All these qualities are intensified by light.

Colours are selected for their relationships, textures for their contrasts. As well as the surface textures of petals and leaves, the overall effect of a flower, or a stem of foliage, can have a textural effect. Chrysanthemums appear rough, for example, although the individual petals are smooth and silky.

Form
Form refers to shape – the outline of a flower. Plant materials have a great variety of shape but can be broadly categorized for the purposes of flower arranging.
ROUND SHAPES are common in flowers – the dahlia, rose, carnation, chrysanthemum and many others are basically rounded in form. They can be used as single or massed elements in an arrangement.
POINTED SHAPES, or spikes, occur in multiple flower stems, such as the

gladiolus and bells of Ireland. These contribute height and linear emphasis to an arrangement.
INTERMEDIATE SHAPES vary from the small Michaelmas daisy to the elegant lily. They provide a link or transition between round and pointed flowers which encourages harmony in a group of mixed flowers.

These forms enhance an arrangement because of their differences. In a massed arrangement, all three shapes are used. In a free-form or line arrangement, one shape may be contrasted with another. Repetition of a single form provides rhythm in a design.

Space
Space between the flowers and within the outline of a design is an important element. In free-form arrangements, space is a particularly positive and integral design element.

The space around an arrangement is also significant. The size and shape of an arrangement is dictated by the space available in the final setting. The space within and around the arrangement should influence the design from the very start and this is closely related to the scale of the setting and the plant materials.

Design principles
Design principles establish the overall impression created by the arrangement for the viewer. These, too, are aimed towards a general sense of harmony in the design. Harmony need not exclude that which is surprising or stimulating, but the presentation must be both interesting and pleasing within the context for which the arrangement is made.

Balance
There are two elements of balance in flower arranging: the physical balance is important – the arrangement should be secure and stable – and the visual balance of the overall shape and style of the arrangement. The following are common reasons for imbalance.
TOP-HEAVY The weight of the arrangement is at the top because large flowers are placed too high.
BOTTOM-HEAVY This occurs because the base used is too large or too deep.
LOPSIDED ANGLE The arrangement

appears to lean to left or right because it is not balanced on a natural axis. Imagine a vertical line through the centre of the arrangement: a balance on either side of this line is not made only by symmetrical placing of materials. A mass of flowers on one side of the line, for example, can be balanced by a more open but extended arrangement of materials on the other side.

Colour, form and texture all contribute to balance. If similar materials are grouped together in one area and contrasted with those in another, there is no linking element which can balance the design visually.

Scale
This is dictated by the relative sizes of every component of the arrangement – base, container, flowers and foliage must all relate to each other in scale. For example, a dahlia would be too large for a specimen vase, a snowdrop too small for a pedestal arrangement, to illustrate the extremes. Careful grading of flower sizes creates a good effect in either a massed arrangement or a linear style. The arrangement must also be in scale with its setting, neither too large nor too insignificant against the surroundings.

Proportion
In simple terms, this is the amount of each individual component. A traditional massed arrangement, for example, should be in the proportion of one-third container to two-thirds flowers. A tall vertical arrangement should stand at least as high as the length of the container.

Texture, shape and colour must also be proportionate. A good arrangement does not have too much of one element. In modern styles, the economical use of just a few flowers creates the impact, while in mixed arrangements, a good distribution of large, medium and small forms, linked colours and contrasting textures produces a successful result.

Rhythm
The arrangement should be constructed so that the eye can run freely over it. Repetition of colour, form and texture, gradations of size and radiating patterns all create a fluid, rhythmical effect, as do strong, flowing curves in a free-form design.

SPRING BASKET

This spring grouping is set in a polythene-lined basket filled with foam, which is covered with reindeer or sphagnum moss. The flowers are grouped as they might be seen in the garden, with tall forsythia at the back and small primulas at the front edge of the basket.

Branches of glycerined pussy willow extend the width at the base of the arrangement.

Overall height: 760mm (30in)	
Width: 710mm (28in)	
SILK MATERIALS	
7 wallflowers (4 dark red, 3 orange)	
9 daffodils	
9 primula plants (3 each blue, pink, yellow)	
9 bluebells	
9 scillas	
5 forsythia branches	
7 crocus	
3 tulips	
NATURAL MATERIALS	
6 glycerined pussy willow stems	

BLOSSOM SPRAY

An interestingly shaped branch provides the basic structure of this arrangement. It is held upright in a ceramic container filled with foam. Buds and mature blossoms are taped to the branch at the points where they might occur naturally. The Japanese parasol creates an appropriate setting.

Briar roses and Chinese lanterns also make a good effect when attached to natural branches.

Overall height: 635mm (25in)	
SILK MATERIALS	
Blossom florets – groups of large and small florets and buds	
NATURAL MATERIAL	
Branch 610mm (24in) long	

91

MIXED FLOWERS

A polychromatic arrangement of mixed flowers from each of the seasons, designed after the style of the Dutch and Flemish schools of painting, is especially suitable for the person who likes to make one or two of each flower species. Many of the flowers described in the step-by-step section are used in this massed arrangement. The butterfly, an attractive detail, is made from silky ribbon coloured with wax crayons. (See page 115.)

Overall height: 915mm (36in)
Width: 815mm (32⅛in)

SILK MATERIALS

Assorted flowers chosen for different size and shapes: one or two of each large and medium-sized flower or branch; three to five of each smaller flower or flower spray

DAFFODILS AND PUSSY WILLOW

To create the elegant curves of this arrangement, stems of pussy willow are carefully bent and secured in a crescent shape in foam fixed off-centre in the rectangular dish. The daffodils are placed as if growing naturally, with the buds at the top, stems of varying lengths radiating from one point and the flowers facing in different directions. The flowing ivy trails give a pleasing balance to the design.

Overall height: 760mm (30in)		
Width: 610mm (24in)		
SILK MATERIALS		
12 pussy willow stems		
3 ivy trails		
7 daffodil flowers		
3 daffodil buds		
10 daffodil leaves		

SHADES OF AUTUMN

For this basket, glowing with autumnal colours, the outline is made with brown beech leaves and Chinese lanterns: clivias provide the focal point. Pompon dahlias and spider chrysanthemums in various oranges, reds and yellows add colour and form, while fuchsias, honesty and Michaelmas daisies complete the arrangement.

A similar basket of summer flowers could be arranged using green beech leaves, roses, poppies and alstroemeria.

Overall height: 760mm (30in)
Width: 900mm (35½in)

SILK MATERIALS

14 beech branches (brown)
2 honesty stems
4 Michaelmas daisies
4 Chinese lantern stems
3 clivia
2 fuchsia
11 spider chrysanthemums (6 yellow, 5 orange)
7 pompon dahlias (three shades of orange)

WINTER LANDSCAPE

This landscape arrangement portrays snowdrops growing, as they do naturally, at the base of a tree. An alder branch with cones and catkins is placed in foam mounted on one side of a piece of slate. The snowdrops are arranged to radiate from the base of the branch, with varying stem lengths and the flowers facing in different directions. Ivy leaves, ferns and fungi are added for textural interest.

Overall height: 380mm (15in)	
Width: 330mm (13in)	
SILK MATERIALS	
10 snowdrops	
5 ferns	
3 ivy leaves	
NATURAL MATERIALS	
2 branches *Alnus glutinosa* (alder)	

HYDRANGEAS AND LENTEN ROSES

A brass coal-scuttle was chosen as the container for these graceful flowers, as the brass lends a warm glow to brighten a dull winter's day and subtly links with the metallic sheen of the hydrangea leaves.

The arrangement is built up using bells of Ireland and eucalyptus to form the outline. Purple hydrangeas form a central axis, flanked by cream hydrangeas and crossed by a diagonal line of lenten roses. Glycerined mahonia leaves provide additional colour and textural interest.

Overall height: 965mm (38in)	
Width: 710mm (28in)	
SILK MATERIALS	
5 bells of Ireland	
6 eucalyptus (3 brown, 3 beige)	
7 hydrangeas (4 beige, 3 purple)	
3 lenten roses	
3 stems rhododendron leaves	
NATURAL MATERIALS	
3 glycerined mahonia leaves	

SPIDER CHRYSANTHEMUMS

Though unsuitable for fresh flowers, the brass ladle is an ideal container for silk flowers, as no water is required. The brass also harmonizes well with the golden colour of the chrysanthemums.

The arrangement is a Hogarth curve, formed by placing the smallest flowers at the outer edges, bending the stems carefully into gentle curves and placing the larger flowers, on shorter stems, towards the centre. Aucuba leaves hide the mechanics and emphasize the focal point.

Overall height: 460mm (18⅛in)	
Width: 230mm (9in)	
SILK MATERIALS	
9 spider chrysanthemums	
6 chrysanthemum leaves	
3 aucuba leaves	

SWEET PEAS

The container is a small modern specimen vase with a piece of foam wedged inside. This light, dainty vase is ideal for the delicate stems of pastel-coloured sweet peas. The flower stems, with leaves and tendrils, are simply placed in the vase in a natural way.

This container is also the perfect choice for displaying a single specimen rose or carnation.

Overall height: 405mm (16in)
Width: 255mm (10in)
SILK MATERIALS
6 sweet pea stems

POPPIES

Glycerined pampas grass and dried grasses are used to create the outline of this all-round arrangement. The container is a brown pottery bowl. The poppies are placed at different heights and angles to fill out the shape, with poppy seedheads, preserved ruscus and brown silk beech leaves interspersed.

This arrangement has a country atmosphere suitable for decorating a large kitchen. Other large bright flowers could be used, such as dahlias or chrysanthemums.

Overall height: 915mm (36in)
Width: 760mm (30in)
SILK MATERIALS
4 beech branches (brown)
14 poppies
NATURAL MATERIALS
15 dried poppy seedheads
Dried and glycerined grasses (fine, heavy and pampas grass)
Dried and glycerined *Ruscus aculeatus*

GERANIUM HALF-BASKET

The wall-mounted half-basket is lined with sphagnum moss and filled with foam. The choice of flowers reflects popular hanging basket selections – fuchsia, geranium, pelargonium and petunia – arranged with trails of ivy and helichrysum. The shades of pink and purple, together with the variety of the flower shapes, blend to give a bright, decorative feature suitable for a porch or patio.

Overall height: 965mm (38in)
Width: 760mm (30in)

SILK MATERIALS
1 fuchsia
11 petunias (pink, pale and dark purple)
5 helichrysum stems
3 geranium plants
3 pelargonium plants
Geranium leaves
6 ivy trails

PEONIES AND GLADIOLI

This traditional triangular
arrangement, set in a rounded pink
jug filled with foam, is outlined with
beech and eucalyptus leaves.
Gladioli give height at the centre
and define the width of the
arrangement, while the peonies
create the main line. Three large
peony leaves conceal the foam and
at the same time emphasize the
focal point. Carnations and
alstroemeria are the transitional
flowers used to fill in. Trails of
variegated ivy complete the effect.

Overall height: 865mm (34in)	
Width: 760mm (30in)	
SILK MATERIALS	
5 gladioli	
7 peonies	
3 carnations	
7 spray carnations	
4 peony leaves	
3 stems grey peony leaves	
2 ivy trails	
6 beech branches	
5 eucalyptus stems	

MAGNOLIA BRANCH

Due to the weight of the branches, firm mechanics are required to anchor the design. This can be achieved by using impact adhesive to glue a pinholder to the base of the container.

Oak branches are used here for their good shape and texture. They are stripped of their leaves before the buds and flowers are attached using brown stem tape. Flower size increases from buds at the branch tips towards the fully open flower which forms the central focus.

Overall height and width: 710mm (28in)	
SILK MATERIALS	
1 large and 7 small magnolia flowers	
5 magnolia buds	
NATURAL MATERIALS	
2 oak branches	

Modern Arrangements

ARUM LILIES

A tall cylindrical container is used here to provide height and vertical emphasis. It is weighted with plasticine or a suitable alternative material and a piece of foam is taped into the container level with the rim.

The arum lilies are arranged in a discreet curve, with the bud at the top and the flowers progressively more open and turned forward as they descend the curve. The arum leaves follow the line and the dried palm leaves add movement and interest. The black and white marbled base is a co-ordinating link between flowers and container.

Overall height: 815mm (32⅛in)	
Width: 350mm (13¾in)	
SILK MATERIALS	
6 arum lilies	
6 arum leaves (2 open and 4 furled)	
NATURAL MATERIALS	
6 dried palm leaves (varying lengths)	

CLIVIA WITH FRESH FOLIAGE

An unusual hand-thrown pottery container, shaped like a claw hammer, harmonizes well with the natural wood background against which the flowers, branches and leaves form a striking crescent display. The container has two placements for flowers, both filled with wet foam taped in place.

Overall height: 760mm (30in)	
Width: 510mm (20⅛in)	

SILK MATERIALS

3 clivia

NATURAL MATERIALS

3 *Arum italicum* 'Pictum' leaves

3 horse chestnut branches

AZALEAS

A sturdy container with a textured finish is made by sticking cork tiles to the sides of a brick, leaving 50mm (2in) of cork standing above the brick to hold dry foam. The azaleas are arranged down a vertical axis, with peony leaves at the base to give visual weight and conceal the mechanics.

The loops are formed from lengths of thin cane; the ends are taped and inserted in the foam. The novelty apple and pear candles are not only pleasing accessories; they form a good colour link.

Overall height: 815mm (32⅛in)
Width: 610mm (24in)
SILK MATERIALS
7 azalea flowers
7 groups azalea leaves
3 peony leaves
NATURAL MATERIALS
3 cane loops

BIRD OF PARADISE FLOWERS

The modern-style container is part of a flue liner, made of a clay composition, obtained from a builder's yard. Its colour blends well with that of the natural dried leaves and it efficiently conceals a well pinholder. Boldly shaped flowers and leaves need a container with weight and clean lines, to balance the design.

The leaves are positioned first and the bright tropical flowers are set in the spaces created by their broad curves.

Overall height: 610mm (24in)	
Width: 710mm (28in)	
SILK MATERIALS	
3 bird of paradise flowers	
NATURAL MATERIALS	
4 dried bird of paradise leaves	

IRIS POOL

A shallow container was chosen to create a natural setting for the iris, the theme accentuated by the ceramic duck and mossy surround. The iris are simply arranged on a vertical axis, inclining slightly in different directions, their naturalness enhanced by the lines of the silk iris leaves.

Overall height: 405mm (16in)	
Width: 355mm (14in)	
SILK MATERIALS	
5 medium-sized iris	
5 iris leaves	

BRONZE CHRYSANTHEMUMS

Texture plays an important part in this design, with each component adding a different and interesting texture. The mechanics are a small well pinholder containing foam. These are mounted on a piece of rough bark and disguised by carefully placed driftwood. The design is an L-shape created by the willow and the base; the flowers are set within this line and large rhododendron leaves emphasize the focal point. Poppies, peonies or hydrangeas could be substituted for the chrysanthemums.

Overall height: 710mm (28in)	
Width: 535mm (21⅛in)	
SILK MATERIALS	
3 bronze chrysanthemums	
NATURAL MATERIALS	
3 rhododendron leaves	
4 *Salix setsuka* stems	

BLACK TULIPS

The container has a very striking shape, with its sweeping curve from left to right. This is emphasized and extended by the line of the black tulips. Their strong, oblique angle threatens to unbalance the design but is offset by the two bold black leaves and the opposing direction of the white tulips.

The strong lines and sharp contrasts of this design would hold their own well against minimalist or high-tech room decor.

Overall height: 510mm (20⅛in)	
Width: 380mm (15in)	
SILK MATERIALS	
4 black tulips	
2 white tulips	
2 black tulip leaves	

PEONIES AND BAMBOO

This simple, stylish arrangement is limited to subtle pinks, creams and greens. A well pinholder with foam stands on the Japanese wickerwork base. The fan is fixed by means of a hairpin of wire passed through the slats of the fan and into the foam.

The curve of the fan leads the eye directly to the peonies and the radiating pattern of the bamboo stems contributes to a well integrated design.

Overall height: 710mm (28in)	
Width: 460mm (18⅛in)	
SILK MATERIALS	
2 peonies	
5 hydrangea leaves	
4 bamboo stems	

NERINES

Dainty nerines are shown to advantage in a glass container, in this case a builders' glass brick. A plastic frog is attached to the glass with impact adhesive. A small piece of foam impaled on the frog and covered with reindeer moss supports the flowers and leaves.

The outline is formed with stems of *Salix 'Tortuosa'* from which the bark has been stripped. Leaves of *Dieffenbachia picta* made of silk have attractive pink markings complementing the flowers.

Overall height: 815mm (32⅛in)	
Width: 405mm (16in)	
SILK MATERIALS	
3 nerines	
3 *Dieffenbachia picta* leaves	
NATURAL MATERIALS	
7 *Salix 'Tortuosa'* stems	

DAHLIAS AND JAPANESE MAPLE

A boldly shaped jar and loose natural style of arrangement make this design suitable for a modern room. The large ceramic jar is weighted with sand for stability; a piece of foam is taped on top of the sand, cut level with the top of the jar.

The maple branches are arranged to form an open, fluid outline, one branch bent over the front of the jar. Begonia leaves, with the stems cut very short, hide the mechanics. The dahlias are loosely inserted, buds at the top and outer edges of the design, full flowers nearer the centre.

Overall height: 1070mm (42¼in)
Width: 560mm (22in)
SILK MATERIALS
6 Japanese maple stems
6 each medium-sized and large dahlias and dahlia buds (3 each light mauve and dark mauve)
3 *Begonia rex* leaves

Christmas Arrangements

CHRISTMAS ROSES

The attractive candle lamp is an integral part of this classically styled Christmas arrangement. The design forms an L-shape, with the Christmas roses following the line to frame the lamp. The flowers and foliage are held in a small watertight dish containing wet foam to maintain the fresh leaves.

Other accessories could be used, such as a snowman, Father Christmas figure or gift parcels. Poinsettias, roses or carnations are flower choices equally suited to the style of the design.

Overall height: 380mm (15in)	
Width: 255mm (10in)	
SILK MATERIALS	
5 Christmas roses	
NATURAL MATERIALS	
Stems of *Cotoneaster salicifolia*, variegated holly, cupressus and ivy	

CHRISTMAS TREE

This tiny Christmas tree is brightened with lanterns, pompon bows and butterflies, decorations made from metallic yarn and poinsettias of metallic silky ribbon. All of these also make attractive decorations for wrapped gifts.

As Christmas decorations are highly inflammable, always be careful to ensure that they are safely, as well as attractively positioned.

A red, silver and green colour scheme creates a traditional Christmas atmosphere.

Overall height: 760mm (30in)	
Width: 510mm (20⅛in)	
SILK MATERIALS	
Poinsettias	
Butterflies and Christmas lanterns	
Ribbon bows	
Metallic yarn bells and holly leaves	
NATURAL MATERIAL	
Container-grown small Christmas tree	

TREE DECORATIONS

BUTTERFLY

TWINKLE DECORATIONS

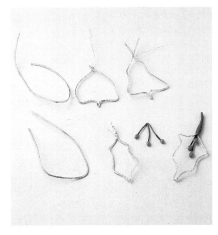

CHRISTMAS LANTERN

MATERIALS
Metallic shaded ribbon
Plain silky ribbon
33- and 24-gauge white covered wires
36mm (1⁷⁄₁₆in) double-sided adhesive tape

MATERIALS
Metallic yarn (silver or gold)
30-gauge wire

Cut lengths of metallic yarn and bend them into decorative shapes such as bells, holly leaves and bows. (The yarn is wired and will stay in shape.) Attach red berry stamens to the holly leaves.

Secure the ends of yarn together with a twist of 30-gauge wire and use this to attach the decorations to Christmas tree branches.

To use the decorations in a flower arrangement, attach the wired tip to a stem wire using stem tape.

MATERIALS
Lantern ribbon
Acetate ribbon
5mm (³⁄₁₆in) double-sided adhesive tape

Cut a piece of silky ribbon and cover with double-sided tape. Trace the butterfly shape on the ribbon and go over the outline with a ballpoint pen.

Peel the backing paper from the double-sided tape and attach 33-gauge white covered wire to the traced outline of the shape. Attach a length of 24-gauge wire through the centre of the butterfly body to form a tail.

Cover the wired outline with metallic shaded ribbon and cut around the butterfly shape.

Alternatively, use all plain silky ribbon and paint patterns on the wings with felt-tip pens.

Cut a 50mm (2in) length of lantern ribbon. Apply double-sided tape to the matt side of the ribbon at top and bottom.

Cut a 48×50mm (1⁷⁄₈×2in) rectangle of acetate ribbon (the colour may match or contrast with the lantern ribbon). Apply double-sided tape to one edge of the acetate rectangle and roll it into a tube shiny side out.

Remove the backing paper from the double-sided tape at the top of the lantern ribbon and attach the edge to the top of the acetate tube. Repeat with the bottom edge.

Place two small pieces of double-sided tape inside the tube and attach a narrow acetate strip or length of metallic yarn about 100mm (3¹⁵⁄₁₆in) long to form a handle.

CHRISTMAS ROSE WREATH

The base of the wreath is a metal coathanger bent into a circle with sphagnum moss tied tightly around it. Alternatively, small blocks of florist's foam wrapped in cling film can be attached to the wire. The evergreen foliage and cones are wired and the wires pushed firmly into the wreath base. For the best effect, add a generous number of Christmas roses and buds.

Overall diameter: 460mm (18⅛in)		
SILK MATERIALS		
14 Christmas roses		
7 Christmas rose buds		
NATURAL MATERIALS		
25-30 pine cones, wired to give 75mm (3in) stems		
Evergreen foliage		

ADVENT WREATH

A plastic wreath ring is the basis of the arrangement, containing wet foam to maintain the fresh evergreens. A red velvet poinsettia forms the focal point at the top of the wreath, linking with the red berries around the circle. More poinsettias could be added for additional colour.

The wreath is quite heavy and the hanging wire should be passed through the foam and bent back around the wreath ring before it is brought up to form a loop.

Overall diameter: 460mm (18⅛in)	
SILK MATERIALS	
1 poinsettia	
NATURAL MATERIALS	
Variegated holly, cupressus (green and variegated) and *Skimmia japonica* all with 75-100mm (3-4in) stems	

TABLE CENTREPIECE

The container, a three-armed candelabra with candle-cup attached to the central arm, suggests the gentle crescent shape of this design. Attach foam to the candle cup and make the crescent with the foliages; position a line of nerines through the curve and add the poinsettias. To mount the central candle, tape wires around the candle at the base and sink these into the foam.

The choice of flowers and foliage suggests a Christmas theme but the basic design would be suitable for any formal dinner party.

Overall height: 405mm (16in)	
Width: 610mm (24in)	
SILK MATERIALS	
3 metallic ribbon poinsettias	
2 nerine buds	
6 nerine flowers	
6 nerine florets	
NATURAL MATERIALS	
Stems of variegated holly, *Lamium*, *Cotoneaster salicifolia*, cupressus and ivy	
Bergenia leaves	

POINSETTIA MIRROR DECORATION

The mechanics of this decoration are a small plastic frog attached to the corner of the mirror supporting a small piece of foam taped in place for extra security. The stem of the large poinsettia is cut very short and pressed into the foam, while the two outer flowers have slightly longer stems. The evergreen foliage is of a type that will last the Christmas period without water.

Overall height: 430mm (17in)	
Width: 305mm (12in)	
SILK MATERIALS	
3 poinsettias	
2 three-looped metallic yarn decorations	
NATURAL MATERIAL	
Cupressus	

BRIDAL BOUQUET AND HEADDRESS

This beautiful bridal bouquet is a mass of delicate colours. The combination of cream, white, peach and pink can be carried against a traditionally styled wedding dress in white or cream. The larger roses are made from both silky and acetate ribbons, to vary the textural detail.

Three trails of varying length are made as explained for a corsage (see page 122) using 18-gauge wire. When the trails are the required length and width, bend the wires at right angles to the trail (the returning end) and complete as instructed for the posy (see page 123).

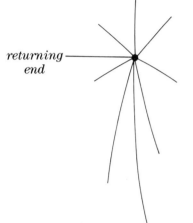

returning end

Overall length: 635mm (25in)	
Width 305mm (12in)	

SILK MATERIALS
All flowers with 305mm (12in) stems

Long trail

5 lily of the valley	
5 rosebuds (varying tones)	
2 freesia stems	
3 freesia florets	
4 rose-leaf trefoils	
2 groups filler flowers	

Small trails

4 lily of the valley	
2 rosebuds	
3 freesia florets	
2 rose-leaf trefoils	
3 groups filler flowers	

Posy

8 rosebuds (mid and deep tones)	
10 small roses (pale and mid tones)	
3 large roses (deep tone)	
10 freesias	
11 freesia florets	
12 rose-leaf trefoils	
20 groups filler flowers	

A headdress to match the bride's bouquet is designed to be worn on the back of the head, attached to the veil. It is made in two sections: lily of the valley, freesias and rosebuds are wired to a 150mm (5⅞in) length of 20-gauge wire, the flowers increasing in size towards the large rose. A 50mm (2in) length of bare wire is left at one end. The second section is made in the same way and the two are joined by overlapping the bare sections of wire and taping them securely. To disguise the join, tape in a central rose and some additional leaves.

Overall length: 460mm (18⅛in)	
Depth: 75mm (3in)	

SILK MATERIALS
All flowers with 50-75mm (2-3in) stems

3 roses	
2 rosebuds	
5 freesia florets	
6 lily of the valley	
8 groups filler flowers	
10 rose leaves	

ORCHID CORSAGE AND BIBLE FLOWERS

Some brides wish to carry a Bible in preference to a bouquet and it is a charming idea to add a flower decoration. A similar arrangement makes a matching corsage. The Bible flowers can be secured by a long wire folded into the book covers, or could be attached to a book mark. Many other flowers are suitable for corsages and small decorations – lilies, roses, freesias, alstroemeria and camellia.

A complementary touch is a white carnation buttonhole for the bridegroom.

A small floret or piece of foliage is taped to a 20-gauge wire and further flowers and leaves are added, gradually widening the trail until it is the desired width for the corsage. The flowers are placed on alternate sides to achieve a good flowing line. Do not use too much tape – two turns between each addition is sufficient. When the trail is the required width place your left thumb at this point (called the returning end) and do not move it until the corsage is completed. Using small flowers and leaves, fix the maximum returning point and the width of the corsage. Add an orchid or other large flower and a ribbon bow to the centre. Twist the wire round the returning end, trim the surplus stems and wrap together securely with stem tape.

Corsage	
Length: 200mm (7⅞in)	
SILK MATERIALS	
Orchid flower and bud	
2 rose leaves	
5 stephanotis	
Ribbon bow	
Bible flowers	
Length: 230mm (9in)	
SILK MATERIALS	
1 orchid	
11 stephanotis	
2 small and 7 large rose leaves	
Each decoration includes natural asparagus fern	

maximum returning point

returning end

122

BRIDESMAID'S BOUQUET AND HEADDRESS

Silk flowers have the advantage over fresh flowers in that they can be made to match the more unusual colours which may be chosen for the bridesmaids' dresses. The colouring of this bouquet and headdress would enhance blue, soft green or cinnamon dress fabrics. White ribbons and posy frills can be dyed with cold water dyes or, in this case, cold tea, to produce the particular hues required.

Five stems of flowers are bent at right angles about 125mm (4^{15}⁄$_{16}$in) from the flowerhead. All stems are held in your hand at the bend (called the returning end) and formed into a five-pointed star. You must hold the returning end until the posy is wired. A central flower is placed perpendicular to the original five stems establishing the height of the posy (about the same as the radius). Fill in with a variety of flowers and foliage and bind together with wire.

Clench the stems in your hand, cut the stem ends slightly below your hand and bind with tape. If a posy frill is required slide the bound stems through the hole in the frill, cover the stems with double-sided adhesive tape and bind with ribbon.

Overall diameter: 255mm (10in)
SILK MATERIALS
20 roses
10 sweet pea flowers
10 hyacinth florets
7 rose-leaf trefoils
(Use a large posy frill to frame the flowers)

The ring for the headdress is formed from a 20-gauge stem wire taped and bent into a hook at one end. As the flowers are added, the wire is bent into a circle. A second hook is made at the other end when complete and the headdress is formed by engaging the two hooks. If a second wire is needed join it in at least 125mm (4^{15}⁄$_{16}$in) from the end of the first wire.

Overall diameter: 240mm (9½in)
SILK MATERIALS
16 roses
8 sweet pea flowers
8 hyacinth florets
32 single rose leaves

TOP-TABLE ARRANGEMENT AND GARLAND

The theme for the top table decoration is linked by using the clematis flowers interspersed with roses in the table centrepiece forming the main element in the garland. Alternatively, the garland could be made with small roses.

The centrepiece includes a variety of fresh foliage which sets off the silk flowers and creates an interesting framework of colour and texture.

The garland is made by wiring silk flowers and leaves together into one continuous length, which is draped gracefully in loops along the front of the tablecloth and pinned in place. Silk flowers are ideal for garland-making, as there is no need to devise a water supply and they can be made well in advance of the event.

Overall height: 510mm (20⅛in)
Width: 760mm (30in)
SILK MATERIALS
9 rosebuds
3 roses
8 spray carnations
4 clematis sprays
5 clematis flowers
NATURAL MATERIALS
Stems of grass, Japanese honeysuckle and 3 *Rosa rubrifolia*
1 *Mahonia japonica* leaf
For the garland
20 clematis flowers
16 groups clematis leaves
2 wired bows

BRIDESMAID'S HOOP

A charming and unusual accessory, the hoop is made from two craft wires covered with stem tape in a colour to tone with the flowers. It may be necessary to tape the wires three or four times to achieve even colouring. Bend the craft wires into semi-circles and tape the ends securely to form a circle. Wire the flowers into a long chain and weave around the hoop. A flourish of fine ribbons completes the effect.

Hoop circumference: 1370mm (54in)
SILK MATERIALS
32 small clematis
24 small groups three leaves
Ribbon bows

POMANDER

The charm of this flower cluster depends upon generous massing of the flowers and ribbons. Thread a hairpin-bent wire through the centre of a 70mm (2¾in) diameter foam ball and bend the ends to form hooks. Pull the hooks back into the foam for anchorage. Use the hairpin loop to secure a ribbon handle. Press the flower stems into the foam ball and angle the flowerheads as if radiating from the centre. Complete with blossom heads and wired ribbon loops and tails.

Diameter: 140mm (5½in)
SILK MATERIALS
14 scabious heads
14-16 blossom florets
14 ribbon loops

TRAINBEARER'S BASKET

The ribbon detail on the handle adds a special touch to this pretty basket. Wind ribbon tightly around the basket handle and finish off with a bow.

The arrangement is designed in complementary colours – yellow and lilac – with a good variety of size and texture. The flowers are all in scale with the container.

Overall height: 200mm (7⅞in)
Width: 255mm (10in)
SILK MATERIALS
3 roses
6 spray carnations
3 clematis
17 blossom florets
6 beech stems (green)
7 ribbon loops

127

WEDDING HEADDRESSES

An Alice-band covered with stem tape in a colour to match the wearer's dress bears three blooms of peach stock wired to one side.

An unusual and attractive headdress can be made with two freesia stems taped together end to end and bent to form an S-shape. This may be attached to a comb or secured in the hair with hairpins.

The white peony is a simple but striking accessory: the size should be carefully calculated to suit the age of the wearer. It is mounted on a short length of taped wire which can be pinned in the hair.

Length: 205mm (8in)
SILK MATERIALS
Top: 2 freesias
Centre: 3 stocks
Below: 1 peony

Church Flowers

PEDESTAL ARRANGEMENT

A pedestal is often used for a church arrangement, as the height is in scale with such surroundings. The pedestal usually stands on the chancel steps, or beside the altar or pulpit.

A flowing triangular outline is created with tall and trailing foliages, gladioli, stock and apple blossom. Lilies and roses form the main line and peonies are set at the centre. Hydrangeas, carnations and aspidistra leaves complete the arrangement.

Overall height: 2135mm (84⅛in)
Width: 1270mm (50in)
SILK MATERIALS
Gladioli, lilies, stocks, blossom, peonies, hydrangeas, rosebuds, roses, carnations and spray carnations, and *Clematis montana*, in pink and white (about 55 flowers in all)
2 ivy trails
8 beech branches
9 aspidistra leaves

CHURCH ENTRANCE FLOWERS

This traditional triangular arrangement includes some lovely and unusual foliages – young raspberry canes, branches of flowering currant and tall spears of *Phormium tenax* – to set off the yellow silk roses. Large flowers at the centre form the focal point, with rosebuds and graceful foliage shaping the outlines of the design.

Overall height: 560m (22⅛in)	
Width: 760mm (30in)	
SILK MATERIALS	
7 rosebuds	
7 roses	
NATURAL MATERIALS	
Mixed foliage including *Phormium tenax*, raspberry canes, *Ribes*, *Bergenia*, *Mahonia japonica*, *Skimmia japonica*, *Buxus sempervirens* , ferns, cupressus	

EASTER LILIES

A low glass dish and half a block of foam form the basis of this strikingly simple arrangement of lilies. Altar flowers should form an attractive and appropriate decoration, while the altar itself remains the focus of attention. To this end, pale-coloured flowers with a clearly defined shape are highly suitable, especially lilies, which are traditionally associated with purity and solemnity.

Overall height: 660mm (26in)	
Width: 610mm (24in)	
SILK MATERIALS	
30 lilies	
12 lily buds	
9 leaves	

SWAG OF ROSES

This arrangement requires a lightweight and unobtrusive container – a plant pot saucer or coffee jar lid can be used. Use a heated stem wire to pierce two holes in the side and thread wire through them to form a loop which can be hung from a pew end or wall bracket. A piece of foam is fixed to a plastic frog and taped firmly to the container, as all the weight of the materials lies to the front of the arrangement.

Decoration of pew ends in a church creates a celebratory atmosphere for a wedding or special festival. At a wedding, the flower colours should co-ordinate with those of the bridal party.

Overall height: 635mm (25in)
Width: 255mm (10in)
SILK MATERIALS
5 rosebuds
3 roses
10 beech branches
9 ribbon loops and 2 ribbon tails

LECTERN DECORATION

Fresh gypsophila and cupressus are used in this arrangement, so the mechanics, though otherwise similar to those on the opposite page, require the use of wet foam.

The cluster of nerines is also suitable for pew end decoration. To provide an appropriate colour choice to suit a special occasion, other medium-sized flowers such as scabious, carnations or alstroemeria could be used in this way.

Overall diameter: 230mm (9in)
SILK MATERIALS
14 nerine florets
Wired ribbon bow
NATURAL MATERIALS
Cupressus, short stems
Gypsophila, short stems

Special Occasions

CHRISTENING CAKE DECORATION

The unusual, delicate colouring of the water lily makes an attractive decoration for a baby boy's christening cake. The stem should be cut as short as possible.

Butterflies in various sizes, made from metallic shaded ribbon (see page 115), are pretty additions to the table decorations and would also be suitable ornaments for a christening gift.

In traditional style, pink ribbons can be used to make these items for the christening of a baby girl.

SILK MATERIALS
1 water lily (white and blue)
3 butterflies

ROSE SPRAY FOR A SINGLE-TIERED WEDDING CAKE

To form the spray, hold the bud and two roses in one hand and curve the stems gently, add the forget-me-nots and rose leaves, and secure the whole with a twist of covered wire set below the largest flower. The neat bow is obtained by wiring the ribbon into shape before it is attached to the spray.

A single rose spray with bow trim decorates the cake knife.

Cake decoration

Overall length: 305mm (12in)	
Width: 150mm (5⅞in)	

SILK MATERIALS

1 briar rose bud	
2 briar roses	
8 groups forget-me-nots	
1 wired bow	

Cake-knife decoration

Overall height and width: 115mm (4½in)	

SILK MATERIALS

1 briar rose	
5 groups forget-me-nots	
4 rose leaves	
1 wired bow	

ROSE ARRANGEMENT FOR A TWO-TIERED WEDDING CAKE

The traditional silver vase holds a petite triangular arrangement, delicate in colour and finely scaled for the container.

The favour at the base of the cake is a spray of rose leaves, small filler flowers and tiny bunches of stamens clustered together and tied with ribbon.

Pretty tulle bonbonnières are decorated with silk flowers and ribbon loops.

Overall height: 230mm (9in)
Width: 150mm (6in)
SILK MATERIALS
3 rosebuds
11 stephanotis
3 blossom sprays
5 rose leaves
3 lily of the valley
NATURAL MATERIAL
Fresh or dried asparagus fern

136

CHRISTMAS CAKE DECORATION

The basis of this small arrangement is a tiny piece of foam. Alternate the metallic holly leaf decorations with real holly leaves to form a circular base and insert the Christmas roses. Fill in with evergreen foliage and red berries.

Cake top

Diameter: 150mm (5⅞in)

SILK MATERIALS

6 Christmas roses

5 metallic yarn holly leaves

1 bunch holly berries

NATURAL MATERIALS

Stems of variegated holly and cupressus

Base decoration

Overall length: 205mm (8in)

SILK MATERIALS

3 Christmas roses

3 twinkle yarn holly leaves

NATURAL MATERIAL

Variegated holly

WATER LILY TABLE CENTRE

Water lilies make an interesting centrepiece for a modern glass-topped table and simply styled tableware. No container is required – the lilies rest on their own stems which are bent together to form a circular base.

An individual place-setting decoration has the novel touch of being also a 'place card': the guest's name is written on the water lily leaf with a silver-ink pen.

Table centre	
Overall height: 205mm (8in)	
Width: 305mm (12in)	
SILK MATERIALS	
6 water lilies (varying sizes) wired to 380mm (15in) stem	
10 leaves	
Place setting	
Medium-sized water lily and one leaf	

Flowers as Gifts

POT PLANTS

Houseplants make colourful gifts for any time of the year – for Mother's Day, Christmas or a housewarming. Pretty china pots are ideal containers. Select the container before you make the plant so you can judge the number of flowers required and the length of the stems.

The stems are secured within the pot either in a hard-drying modelling compound or in dry foam.

Pelargonium

Overall height: 175mm (6⅞in)	
Width: 230mm (9in)	
SILK MATERIALS	
1 each five- and four-floret flower stems	
2 three-floret flower stems	
12 small and 6 each medium and large leaves	

Cyclamen

Overall height: 230mm (9in)	
Width: 150mm (5⅞in)	
SILK MATERIALS	
7 flowers	
3 each open and unopened buds	
21 leaves	

African Violet

Overall height: 150mm (5⅞in)	
Width: 125mm (4¹⁵⁄₁₆in)	
SILK MATERIALS	
13 flowers	
5 buds	
24 leaves	

SHELL DECORATIONS

Lily of the valley, roses and sweet peas make simple and beautiful Mother's Day gifts. The flowers are held in the decorative shells by a small piece of modelling compound in which the flower stems are inserted. These simple mechanics make the shells ideal gifts for children to arrange.

Lily of the valley is particularly well complemented by asparagus fern, which can be obtained fresh or dried from a florist.

Height and width to suit shell base	
SILK MATERIALS	
1 sweet pea	
1 rosebud	
3 lily of the valley	
NATURAL MATERIAL	
Asparagus fern	

EASTER BASKET

This charming basket was chosen as the container for its resemblance to a bird's nest. Filled with eggs, it is decorated with yellow chicks and velvety yellow pansies. These are secured by threading the stem wires through the basketwork and bending them behind the handle.

As an Easter gift for a child, or as a family present, fill the basket with chocolate eggs. Primulas, daffodils or forget-me-nots are suitable alternative choices for the flower decoration.

Overall diameter: 255mm (10in)
SILK MATERIALS
5 pansies (varying stem lengths)

HYACINTH BOWL

A hyacinth bowl is a popular present and this one will not fade. For a good effect, the flower stems must be upright and firmly secured in place. The taped end of each stem is split to form a fork and inserted in a block of foam. The foam is concealed with a layer of peat.

An old soup tureen with period decoration is an excellent container; plastic or ceramic bulb bowls are good alternatives.

Overall height: 355mm (14in)	
Width: 305mm (12in)	
SILK MATERIALS	
3 hyacinths	
12 leaves	

IRIS IN A PASTA JAR

As a useful and attractive Mother's Day or housewarming gift, the pasta jar could contain roses, tulips or alstroemeria, in colours chosen to match the kitchen scheme.

To place the iris in the jar, hold them in your hand with the flowerheads at varying heights, bend the stems to form a circular base and slide the flowers into the jar. The pompon bow is tied to the lid and the ribbon wrapped around and down the jar, secured at the base with adhesive or double-sided tape.

Overall height:
460mm (18⅛in)
SILK MATERIALS
3 miniature iris
Pompon bow

COATHANGER AND POT-POURRI SACHET

Satin and lace provide these useful gifts with an aura of luxury and delicate silk flowers contribute a specially personal touch.

The camellia buds are wired to the coathanger hook. Blossom heads with stems cut very short are simply attached to the pot-pourri sachet and powder puff with flowermaking adhesive.

SILK MATERIALS
2 camellia buds
4 blossom florets

LAMPSHADE AND PHOTO-FRAME FLOWER SPRAYS

Flower decorations personalize gifts like these and can be simple to make. The trail of flowers for the lampshade consists of fuchsias and ivy leaves taped to a strong but pliable wire – 26-gauge is suitable – leaving a length of covered wire at either end to be twisted together inside the lampshade.

The small frame decoration, making a co-ordinated set for a bedside table or dressing table, is secured with flowermaking adhesive.

Lampshade spray
Overall length: 230mm (9in)
SILK MATERIALS
4 fuchsia
10 ivy leaves
Picture frame
SILK MATERIALS
1 fuchsia
2 ivy leaves

Haircomb sprays These are only three variations of pretty comb decorations which can be quickly made to add a special accessory to summer dresses or party wear. The pearly stamens of the hyacinth blossoms are partly concealed within the flower; long pearl stamens are an elegant addition to tooled fuchsia pink florets; spring blossoms have a fresh effect.

A twist of covered wire holds the flowers in a small spray and is passed through the teeth of the comb and twisted to secure.

SILK MATERIALS
Top: 5 blossom florets
Centre: 6 heads filler flowers
Bottom: 6 hyacinth florets

Flowers for a straw hat A poppy is ideal decoration for a straw hat worn to a garden party or summer wedding. Sweet peas are another pleasantly informal ornament. Roses, with all their variety of colour, are suited to formal and informal occasions of all kinds.

A camellia is a sophisticated ornament for a broad-brimmed straw hat. It can be pinned in place or secured with flowermaking adhesive.

SILK MATERIAL
1 poppy

Cocktail rose Black silky ribbon creates a stylish and luxurious accessory for a cocktail dress; alternatively, it can be attached to a slimline clutch bag or evening purse or a plainly styled hat.

SILK MATERIALS
1 black rose
5 rose leaves

144